ENDORSEMENTS FOR THE BATTLE—DAVID DUSEK

"Perfectly titled, *The Battle* by David Dusek goes straight to the heart of issues facing today's Christian men. Illustrating the precepts of biblical manhood in the context of a legendary battle during the Vietnam war, makes this book appealing and powerful. After reading it, you'll want to give a copy to all the men and boys in your life. This book is a keeper."

—LtCol Oliver L. North USMC (Ret), bestselling author of *The Rifleman* and host of the Real American Heroes podcast.

"Great stories often teach great life lessons. Such is the case in David Dusek's book, *The Battle*, detailing the fight at Ia Drang, Vietnam. Riveting and compelling, David has done a masterful job of using this story to open our eyes as men to the spiritual fight we are in. But even more important, he shows us through military metaphors, how to win at manhood. Highly practical; I highly recommend it."

—Dr. Robert Lewis, author, Men's Fraternity Founding Partner, BetterMan

"*The Battle* is an incredible book with great content. David Dusek does an exceptional job of capturing what it looks like to tackle life involving multiple aspects. He puts his wisdom to paper as he enlightens his readers on how to succeed at life. This book will leave a lasting impression on the reader and equip them with the necessary tools to continue in their journey."

—Joe White, president, Kanakuk Kamps,
PromiseKeepers keynote speaker

"Custer could have used this book and would likely have lived longer and better. His 20th century successor, Hal Moore, did use its principles when commanding the same 7th Cavalry in Vietnam. This book is something of a pre-fight battle brief written by one rough cut man to other rough cut guys—how to survive on a planet at war against everything you hold dear.

"No matter where you look, life is a battle. From the first pages of Genesis thru the final chapters of Revelation, the Bible is replete with the vocabulary of war. War is probably the single greatest constant in earth history. So how does a guy survive? David Dusek provides some direction: Know your enemy; keep your kit at the ready; Stay together; Never quit.

"Our God loves manly warriors. His Bible is full of them and His own Son is the best who ever lived! Jesus defeated the devil on the high ground of Calvary. And the apostle Paul summarized his own Christian life as a 'good fight.' So kit up, guys, and get in the fight, to win."

—Stu Weber. pastor and author of *Tender Warriors*
and *Four Pillars of a Man's Heart*

The Battle

Tactics for Biblical Manhood Learned from the 7th Cavalry in Vietnam

By
David Dusek

FIDELIS
PUBLISHING

FIDELIS PUBLISHING
ISBN: 978-1-7354285-6-7
ISBN (eBook): 978-1-7354285-7-4

The Battle
Tactics for Biblical Manhood Learned from the 7th Cavalry in Vietnam
© 2021 David Dusek

Cover Design by Diana Lawrence
Interior Design by Xcel Graphic

All rights reserved, including the right to reproduce this book or
portions thereof in any form whatsoever. For information, address info@
fidelispublishing.com.

No part of this publication may be reproduced or transmitted in any form or
by any means electronic or mechanical, including photocopy, recording, or any
information storage and retrieval system now known or to be invented, without
permission in writing from the publisher, except by a reviewer who wishes
to quote brief passages in connection with a review written for inclusion in a
magazine, newspaper, website, or broadcast.

For information about special discounts for bulk purchases, please contact
BulkBooks.com, call 1-888-959-5153 or email - cs@bulkbooks.com

Unless otherwise indicated all Scripture comes from Holy Bible, New
International Version®, NIV® Copyright ©1973, 1978, 1984, 2011 by Biblica,
Inc.® Used by permission. All rights reserved worldwide.

(NLT) New Living Translation - Holy Bible, New Living Translation,
copyright © 1996, 2004, 2015 by Tyndale House Foundation. Used by
permission of Tyndale House Publishers, Inc., Carol Stream, Illinois 60188. All
rights reserved.

(ESV) English Standard Version - The Holy Bible, English Standard Version.
ESV® Text Edition: 2016. Copyright © 2001 by Crossway Bibles, a publishing
ministry of Good News Publishers.

(KJV) King James Version is in the public domain.

Fidelis Publishing, LLC Sterling, VA • Nashville, TN
fidelispublishing.com
Manufactured in the United States of America
10 9 8 7 6 5 4 3 2

CONTENTS

This book is dedicated to the memory of LTG Harold G. Moore, CSM Basil Plumley and to the men of the U.S. Army's 1st Battalion of the 7th U.S. Cavalry (Airmobile), who fought valiantly in the Ia Drang Valley of South Vietnam on 14–17 November 1965.

For the families of those Troopers who didn't make it home, and for the men who did, thank you. It is an honor to know you and a privilege to call many of you my friends.

Garryowen!

FOREWORD

Activated in 1861, the U.S. Army's 7th Cavalry Regiment has an incredible history of service to the nation. Most Americans remember it as the unit George A. Custer commanded at the Battle of Little Bighorn River during the fight against Sitting Bull and his Sioux warriors in June 1876. Also known as "Custer's Last Stand," this battle has been immortalized in movies and numerous books. Young lads have enjoyed recreating the battle in make-believe fights against hostile Indians for over a century. The 7th Cavalry Regiment also served during the Philippine-American war, as well as in Cuba during the Spanish-American War. World War II and Korea found the 7th Cavalry fighting in the Pacific Theater, where it once again produced a distinguished combat record.

Less than a century after the battle of Little Bighorn and Custer's demise, the 7th Cavalry was thrust into an incredible fight where they were severely outnumbered by the enemy. The battle of the Ia Drang Valley in Viet Nam on November 14,1965 would become another legendary fight for the 7th

Cavalry. It is remembered as the first major encounter by U.S. Forces in Viet Nam with the North Vietnamese Army (NVA). Commanding the 1st Battalion, 7th Cavalry Regiment during this three-day battle was LTC Harold G. Moore. Moore was a U.S. Military Academy graduate (1945) where he prepared for a life of leading men in the U.S. Army. West Point taught Hal Moore discipline and commitment. There he developed into a fine soldier and an outstanding leader. As the battle of the Ia Drang Valley unfolded, it was the leadership skills of Hal Moore that prevented this from being a total annihilation of the 7th Cavalry Regiment.

One evening in 2006, I met with LTG Moore for dinner in Washington, DC. It was a great honor just to be in his presence. At the time, he was eighty-four years old but looked and spoke like a much younger man. He was impressive as he shared bits and pieces of his life as a soldier with me and a couple of friends. What became clear very quickly was Hal Moore was a man of faith. His love of God and his reliance upon the Creator throughout his career was a theme of his discussion that night.

I found myself wondering what it would have been like to have served under this great man, particularly in the battle of the Ia Drang Valley. Given that LTG (Ret.) Moore was a soldier for over three decades and led men in combat in some of the toughest fights in the last half of the Twentieth Century, it should be obvious his knowledge, wisdom, and life lessons must be passed from generation to generation and shared with as many men as possible. And that is exactly what David Dusek has done.

As Christians, we should know warfare is a constant in our lives. We are at war but it is not always a physical war. Rather, it is generally spiritual warfare. But how many Christians really understand spiritual warfare? Few pastors discuss spiritual warfare or preach about it. It is not a popular topic to speak about, so it is often avoided, leaving Christians rather unprepared for what they face every day as a believer in and follower of Jesus Christ. Exodus 15:3 is very clear, "the Lord is a warrior, the Lord is His name" (NIV). Furthermore, Revelation 19 describes Jesus as a warrior returning to earth with the weapons of warfare and leading a mighty army into battle against His enemies. So it makes sense that God's expectation of every Christian is they are warriors in His Kingdom here on earth and they are engaged every day with the evil inhabiting our world.

Yet how many of us are prepared for battle? How many of us know how the enemy of God operates, or better stated, how many of us know his tactics? Hal Moore knew the tactics of the NVA regulars and therefore was able to achieve victory against them. Today, most men are conflicted and confused over what a man is supposed to be because we live in a society that does not value moral courage or the warrior ethos the way one would expect. When a man steps into battle against the forces of evil, it requires knowledge, skill, and courage to be victorious. Like Hal Moore, a man must be adequately prepared for all the tricks and deception a wily enemy can throw at him.

In this book, *The Manhood Battle*, David Dusek uses the battle experiences of then-LTC Moore and the 1st Battalion, 7th Cavalry as a guide to understanding spiritual warfare and to preparing for and engaging in it. This is a "How-To" handbook to knowing the enemy and knowing how to be on the winning side of every engagement with the devil.

David Dusek spent many hours before writing *The Manhood Battle* interviewing the men under Moore's command in the Ia Drang Valley. His interviews are almost mesmerizing. David shares the lessons learned by the men who were there with the reader as he compares the tenets of spiritual warfare with those of physical combat like that experienced by Moore and his men. The tactics, techniques, and procedures (TTP's) used by the men of the 7th Cavalry apply in the spiritual realm as well. David has done a masterful job here showing how men can and should use the same TTPs in their daily walk with Christ.

Take a journey with Hal Moore and the men of the 7th Cavalry and experience the Ia Drang fight from a spiritual perspective.

LTG (Ret.) William G. Boykin, U.S. Army
Delta Force, U.S. Army Special Operations Command
Executive Director–Family Research Council

INTRODUCTION

I f you've read my first book, *Rough Cut Men*, my passion for movies isn't a shocker. Nor is my love for everything and anything *We Were Soldiers*. There's something so compelling about an outnumbered unit of soldiers facing an unknown enemy and beating the odds. It's in every guy's DNA to root for the underdog, even when we don't realize we're the underdog until the battle starts. I know this first hand. I'm a Florida Gators football fan.

So when God prompted me to write a book about this "Army cultural phenomenon" known as the "Battle of Ia Drang," I was pumped! After all, I use action movie sequences in the live *Rough Cut Men* events and thought it would be great to incorporate more *We Were Soldiers* into it. You'd be hard-pressed to find a soldier on the planet who isn't familiar with the likes of then-LTC Hal Moore, CSM Basil Plumley or the cast of characters of the 1st Battalion of the 7th U.S. Cavalry (Airmobile), circa 1965. And you'd be equally hard-pressed to find regular guys like me who haven't seen the movie or read the book *We Were Soldiers Once . . . And Young,* the official recount of the battle co-authored by Moore and UPI reporter Joseph Galloway.

November 14, 2012. Ironically, the 47th anniversary of the commencement of the three-day battle that left seventy-nine troopers from the 1/7 dead and another 121 wounded, I was in the bathroom (too much information?), where most of us guys do our best thinking. While contemplating putting up a commemorative Facebook post about the anniversary, God clearly told me to write about it. And not just blog about it but write a book about it. I thought to myself, "That's a great idea!"

Precisely eight seconds later, I thought, "Really, God? You want me to write a book about a movie based on a book? I think that's plagiarism." Dismissing the whole deal, I hit the laptop for my usual work. *Find Joe Galloway* I hear in my head. Excuse me? I mean, one doesn't simply "find" Joe Galloway. He's a journalistic and photographic icon and a personal hero of mine. *Find Joe Galloway* I hear again. So I Googled Joe and found the usual plethora of articles about him. Then, deep into the far reaches of cyberspace, I find his agent's name and number and I make the call. After all, if God's behind it, maybe it'll work, right?

Long story short, within an hour, I was on the phone with *the* Joe Galloway. After overcoming being acutely star-struck, we set a time to meet when I was in his home town. Shortly thereafter, I was given now-LTG Hal Moore's address and wrote him a letter. On fire now, I wrote letters to all the actors in the movie to find out just what Moore was like as a man.

Then the voice of reason, aka my accountability partner, chimed in. He said, "You can't write a book about a man based on the opinion of the man himself. You need to find out what his subordinates thought about him." Great. Now I have to track down everybody?

I quickly got to work, connecting with a friend at West Point and soon garnered the contact information of Moore's

Company commanders. And just to show you how God works, one of the men, Alpha Company Commander Tony Nadal invited my wife and me to the reunion of Landing Zone X-Ray to meet everyone!

Finally, after several months, I received word from one of Hal Moore's sons, "The General" (as most called him) wasn't doing well physically at ninety-plus years old. While that may seem disappointing on the surface, I gained the unique opportunity to interview several of Moore's children and even his granddaughter.

In February of 2017, LTG Harold G. Moore moved on to Glory with Jesus and I was privileged to attend both his Funeral Mass in his hometown of Auburn, Alabama, as well as his Memorial Celebration held at the National Infantry Museum at Fort Benning.

What you hold in your hand is a compilation of several years of hard labor. You're going to find movie references—of course, given I talk in movie quotes all the time—interviews from the aforementioned folks, and principles learned on the battlefield.

In a nutshell, this is a handbook designed to equip you to be the absolute best leader you can be, learned from both the Army career and the personal life of Hal Moore, the men who served under him in combat, and the strategies used in one three-day battle in the Central Highlands of Vietnam.

Bottom line up front, we are leaders. We are the men of God's army. And we are soldiers, too.

Let's get in the fight! It's time to engage!

A QUICK HISTORY LESSON—VERY QUICK

The Vietnam War has always received a really bad rap, whether from the kind folks who spit on soldiers returning home back in the 1970's or even more recently from Hollywood, who often depicts soldiers from the Vietnam era as crazy, psychotic stoners who "killed babies." Just take a look at *Apocalypse Now* or *Hamburger Hill* if you don't believe me.

However, the men of the 1st Battalion of the 7th U.S. Cavalry (Airmobile) were, and are, anything but how cinema portrays Vietnam, and the mere thought of anyone spitting on these men brings me to a rolling boil in about thirty seconds. I know them, I know their families, and I know the battle. And I'd like to introduce you to some of them, starting with the genesis of how they all ended up together in that South Vietnamese river valley in 1965.

By the way, I speak in bullets most of the time, so I'm going to unpack this very quick lesson in Vietnam War history in the same fashion. The information is necessary to tee up the rest of the book and the cast of characters in it. If you've seen the movie, *We Were Soldiers*, many of the men who were actually there say the movie is about 70 percent accurate (which isn't bad by movie standards). I'm shooting for 90 percent accurate, which isn't bad for me. But I promise there won't be a test at the end.

- During the early 1960's, Vietnam was plagued with coup after counter-coup as North Vietnam, consisting of both People's Army of North Vietnam (PAVN) and Viet Cong fighters of South Vietnam (VC) overtook the much-weaker Army of the Republic of Vietnam (ARVN) of South Vietnam
- At this point, American combat activity in Vietnam was limited to the use of CIA and "Advisors," sent in to strike the PAVN/VC and assist in ARVN training, respectively
- By early 1965, as the VC gained limited control of South Vietnam, U.S. Army General Westmoreland secured a commitment of roughly 300,000 U.S. troops. Westmoreland was merely waiting for the appropriate time to mobilize the U.S. Army "regulars"
- By 1965, the VC and PAVN troops were in control of the Central Highlands, northeast of Saigon, an area with few roads. The area was critical, as North Vietnam was poised to literally cut South Vietnam in half
- Because of the relative impassability of the terrain, the Army decided this would be an outstanding location to test new air-assault technology, as traditional ground elements, tanks, and heavy equipment would be unable to reach the AO (Area of Operations)
- The new air assault unit, originally tasked as the "11th Air Assault Division (Test)" but later re-numbered the "1st Cavalry Division (Airmobile)," would deliver battalion-sized elements into the theater using UH-1 helicopters, backed up by close air support from both fighter aircraft and

helicopter-mounted ARA (Aerial Rocket Artillery), and strategically placed .105mm Howitzer artillery batteries

- The Battle of Ia Drang (named after the river located in the valley) was the first major clash between 'regular' soldiers of the U.S. Army and the People's Army of Vietnam during the war
- The battle at Landing Zone X-Ray (LZ X-Ray) took place on November 14–16, 1965, as part of the U.S. airmobile offensive code-named 'Operation Silver Bayonet'
- 3rd Brigade, 1st Cavalry Division commander, Colonel Thomas 'Tim' Brown, selected Lt. Colonel Harold G. 'Hal' Moore, commander of the 1st Battalion of the 7th Cavalry Regiment, to handle the mission into the Ia Drang Valley
- Moore's orders were simple. Take roughly 450 men (out of the 765 battalion-authorized strength) to LZ X-Ray, find the enemy, and kill them
- The 1st Battalion of the 7th Cavalry, or '1/7', consisted of three rifle companies. Alpha Company, under the command of Captain Tony Nadal, Bravo Company, under the command of Captain John Herren, and Charlie Company, commanded by Captain Bob Edwards. One heavy weapons company, D Company, under the command of Captain Ray Lefebvre, consisted of mortar, machine gun, and recon units
- The Command Sergeant Major of the battalion was CSM Basil Plumley, a paratrooper who'd already seen action in both World War II and Korea
- LZ X-Ray was roughly the size of a football field and it was determined prior to the battle, only eight Hueys could fit in the LZ at any given time. Each Huey was able to transport between ten to twelve battle-ready soldiers at a time, which meant several "lifts" were needed to move each company into the area

- Additionally, the 1st Cavalry base of operations at Plei Me was fourteen miles from the LZ, meaning significant time (nearly thirty minutes) between lifts
- The first troopers on the ground at LZ X-Ray were Bravo Company and Headquarters, followed by Alpha, Charlie, and finally, Delta
- Lastly, the soldiers were joined on the battlefield by a UPI war correspondent from Refugio, Texas named Joe Galloway, who ultimately co-authored the book *We Were Soldiers Once, And Young*
- What was unknown at the outset of the mission was, in the Chu Pong mountains immediately adjacent to LZ X-Ray, there were three divisions of enemy troops (roughly 1600 men) who wanted to "kill American's very badly," but just hadn't found any yet
- You'll see the word "Garryowen" every so often. It's even on the 1/7 CAV unit patch. Garryowen is actually an Irish tune for quickstep song, which was originally selected by General George Custer as the 7th Cavalry marching tune. And it's been the call sign of the 7th Cavalry ever since.

I'm stopping right here and I will download the rest of the information about the battle at LZ X-Ray in pieces from here on out. But now the stage is set, right?

CHAPTER

WAR

After years of recollection and writing, Lt. General Hal Moore and Joe Galloway penned the book *We Were Soldiers Once, and Young*, completing the work in 1992. I've spent some time with Joe in Charlotte, North Carolina, usually picking his brain about writing, publishing, and obviously his career as a war correspondent. I knew he would be a tremendous resource as I tried to merge movie clips, interview material, book quotes, and battle history into one book. The thought of trying to keep everything in correct order, while achieving maximum impact was killing me. Overwhelmed, I remember asking him how he managed to seamlessly merge all the information on 450 men and the battle chronology, after twenty-five years. He said, "Easy. Just cut and paste." I sat there, thinking the limits of being able to see less than a page at a time on my computer screen wouldn't help when cutting and pasting from hundreds of MS Word pages.

Voicing my confusion, Joe responded with, "No. Cut and paste. Take every page you have, lay it all out on the floor and cut the pages and paste them together in order." Ah, the limits of a computer mind. It made perfect sense.

When I questioned Joe about simply remembering details of a seventy-two-hour battle, several decades in the past, coupled with the fog of war, he said it was a team effort. "When I'd get stuck writing, I'd yell to the General in the other room, 'Hal, which guy was in this particular position?' or 'What was that Troopers name?' That guy can remember every detail."

A decade later, the movie *We Were Soldiers* hit the theater, with Mel Gibson starring as Moore, Barry Pepper portraying Joe, and Sam Elliott taking on the role of CSM Plumley. By the way, the word is Elliott actually underplayed Plumley. Having missed the chance to meet the Sergeant Major, who passed away in October 2012, I can't imagine anyone being a better NCO than the one Elliott plays so well.

There is an incredible speech delivered by Moore in the movie, set on a Doughboy Field at Fort Benning prior to the 1/7 deploying to Vietnam. It's what is said in the scene, as Moore addresses his entire unit, that's the inspiration for this book.

Everyone is in full dress uniforms, with Hueys overhead and families in the grandstand, as Moore addresses the 1st Battalion of the 7th Cavalry:

> *Look around you. In the 7th Cavalry, we've got a captain from the Ukraine; another from Puerto Rico. We've got Japanese, Chinese, Blacks, Hispanics, Cherokee Indians. Jews and Gentiles. All Americans. Now here in the states, some of you in this unit may have experienced discrimination because of race or creed. But for you and me now, all that is gone. We're moving into the valley of the shadow of death, where you will watch the back of the man next to you, as he will watch yours. And you won't care what color he is, or by what name he calls God. They say we're leaving home. We're going to what home was*

always supposed to be. Now let us understand the situation. We are going into battle against a tough and determined enemy. I can't promise you that I will bring you all home alive. But this I swear, before you and before Almighty God, that when we go into battle, I will be the first to set foot on the field, and I will be the last to step off, and I will leave no one behind. Dead or alive, we will all come home together. So help me, God.

Is it just me or does that speech fire you up, too? I love this guy! Granted, the real Hal Moore delivered this briefing in a small unit gathering aboard the Merchant Marine vessel transporting the Battalion from Charleston, SC to Southeast Asia. Randal Wallace, who also directed Gibson in *Braveheart* opted to set the address on the field for cinematic effect. Moore was the consummate leader nonetheless and the text of his speech remains nearly unaltered from the original meeting.

What I didn't realize, until I started talking with both Moore's subordinates from the battle and his own children, is virtually everything Hal Moore did as a soldier, he also did at home as a husband and father.

Let me say that one more time:

Everything Hal Moore did as a soldier, he also did at home as a husband and father.

We may not be in Vietnam, or Afghanistan, but make no mistake:

WE ARE AT WAR.

It's really simple. Just look at the following verse from the Bible.

The thief comes only to steal and kill and destroy—John 10:10a

See what I mean? We have an enemy who wants to kill us. If he can kill us, he can kill our family. He's just sitting out there, looking for a way to take us out. You don't need a theology degree to get a lucid description of the enemy and his mission.

The Apostle Paul painted a great picture of our battlefield in a letter to the folks in Ephesus:

For our struggle is not against flesh and blood, but against the rulers, against the authorities, against the powers of this dark world and against the spiritual forces of evil in the heavenly realms.

Ephesians 6:12

The trick to defeating the enemy is to shoot him before he shoots you, anticipate his next move, stay covered, and occasionally even overwhelm him with so much firepower he can't survive.

Think like the enemy and live to fight another day. Put solid men around you to cover your "six" (aka- backside). Win. It worked in combat in 1965, and it will work for us as men in the world today.

WE ARE THE TARGET

When our soldiers first made contact with the regular army of North Vietnam, they had no idea who they were facing. Fortunately, at least initially, the bad guys didn't know much about our tactics either. They'd never engaged each other, so the learning curve was huge on both sides. I'm told, upon their first exposure to helicopters, some of the OPFOR (Opposing Force) thought the chopper was a flying locomotive of some sort, since the noise was completely foreign and deafening. Some of the locals have been said to have even called them "Train Soldiers."

On our side, the U.S. Army had never gone toe-to-toe with men they couldn't see, as the PAVN soldiers were guerilla warfare experts who often capitalized on their surroundings. Tactically, the longer the Vietnam War dragged on, the more often our soldiers encountered new weapons of warfare like booby traps, trip wires tied to grenades, and pits filled with sharpened, and sometimes poisoned, sticks. Knowing the sound of a Soviet-made AK-47 was one thing but falling into a brush-covered punji pit was something completely new. To make matters worse, many of our guys were taken out of the battle before even firing a shot due to jungle diseases like Malaria or were quickly removed from the field because of jungle rot, which stemmed from being constantly damp because of the high humidity and long monsoon rainy seasons.

As in prior wars, time enabled both armies to understand how the other side operated and to evolve and adapt accordingly. But at the outset, combat was trial by fire, literally. Tactically, our soldiers did what they were trained to do in previous campaigns and the enemy soon discovered some pretty solid ways to attack our men. Predictably, fighting a ground war using tactics from World War II were not going to work against, as one character in the movie called them, "cavemen in black pajamas." Southeast Asia was a completely new theater of operations requiring a completely new playbook.

At the genesis of the Vietnam War, we would march columns of troops through nearly impassable jungle terrain, where both the NVA and PAVN troops would wreak havoc on our guys by adhering to a singular plan of attack—ambush. And while the enemy knew little about our overall military tactics, the "bad guys" figured out three valuable targets pretty quickly.

The first person the enemy would put his crosshairs on was the soldier with the little white or black symbol on his helmet. This guy was definitely a person you should shoot at. He was the officer—the leader. Whether a "butterbar" Second Lieutenant platoon leader, or a battalion-commanding Lt. Colonel, the enemy concluded that taking the leader down had an immediate impact on the rest of the soldiers. If only for a moment, the loss of a leader throws off the dynamics of the mission. After all, the commander has the maps, the battle plans, and the marching orders for the entire unit. Fortunately, our guys figured out that those insignias of rank on helmets were a bad idea, so it wasn't too long before every soldier's helmet looked the same. No one saluted anyone in the field either, as it would be a dead giveaway an officer was somewhere in the rank and file.

An interesting side note revolves around the 1st Cavalry Division logo as well. If you've never seen it, it's a bright yellow shield, with a black diagonal bar running from the upper left to the lower right and a horse head silhouette in the upper right corner.

Yes, that's right, I said bright yellow. Imagine for a moment hundreds of U.S. soldiers, dressed for maximum stealth in their BDU's (Battle Dress Uniforms). They're in green camouflage from head to foot to blend with the surroundings but emblazoned on their shoulders was this bright yellow patch. I can only speculate on the number of shoulder injuries with that yellow target running through the jungle. Let's just say this feature also changed pretty quickly, to a matching green unit patch.

The second man the enemy would aim for was the soldier with an M-60 machine gun on his shoulder and his accompanying ammo man. The machine gunner was pretty hard to miss, given the size of his weapon. The PAVN army took a particular interest in neutralizing these men, since the magnitude of damage caused by a 7.62-mm machine gun firing roughly 500 rounds per minute, up to 1000 yards away, was pretty catastrophic. It became quite common for the machine gunner to go down within minutes of jumping out of a Huey, with the average life expectancy of said machine gunner hovering right around seventeen seconds after firing the first round. Sure, they could do unparalleled damage with that gun, but many didn't live long enough to burn through one belt of ammo.

And then there was the radio operator, the third target on the enemy hit list. He was the soldier with the giant antenna sticking up out of his backpack, which made him as obvious as a machine gunner. You'd usually find the "comms guy" running behind another guy shouting orders into a handset. And since the handset and radio were connected by a long cord, the radio operator often looked a lot like a little dog being dragged for a high-speed walk by his owner.

The enemy wouldn't just shoot the radio operator, either. They would shoot through the radio itself, because anyone could pick it up and use it. The reason is simple enough and likely doesn't need a lot of explanation. If a unit can't communicate, they can't fight. Not only does the lack of a radio create issues in ground communications from platoon to platoon, but it also effectively severs all lines from the fighting forces on the ground to the close air support, the forward operating base, artillery fire support officers, and even medevac teams. The loss of a radio can be crippling to troops in the field.

Now, while we are certainly not being shot at by hostiles in the literal sense of the word, we can certainly learn a lot from the operational successes of the enemy soldiers in Vietnam. And I sure don't want to minimize what our soldiers do in battle by comparing life to war. But at the very least, we can learn much from those who fought and died as we engage in the battle of life.

Contrary to popular culture these days, men are called to be the spiritual leader in the home. The Apostle Paul even went so far as to say *"For a husband is the head of his wife as Christ is the head of the church. He is the Savior of his body, the church."* (Eph 5:23 NLT). And the man's role as leader doesn't just stop at the threshold of our homes but should impact the church, the marketplace, the community, and even the world. If you haven't noticed, our wives are typically responders, who are usually just following our lead whether it be relational or emotional. We can keep peace in the home, or we can create havoc by merely speaking the wrong thing at the wrong time.

I'm always acutely aware that I can either build my wife up or rob her joy within seconds of walking through the door.

Remember, *"The tongue has the power of life and death"* (Proverbs 18:21) and we have the capability, as the leader, to build up morale at home, or virtually level it with our words. God has tapped us as the head of the household, not to be a tyrannical leader but a gentle shepherd who lovingly leads our family, stewards our marriage and our finances, and trains our children to follow the Lord. Where we lead, they will likely follow, for better or worse

That being said, in the grand "formation" of an army at home, we are the guy with that little battlefield emblem on our helmet. We are the officer. And to that end, based upon the tactic of "Kill the leader, kill the unit," we are invariably the primary target of the enemy. If Satan wants to take down a marriage, he takes out the husband. If the parents ultimately divorce, many kids will go down, and some are even lost for good. Then the family legacy dives into a flat spin and the enemy has won multiple generations through the failure of one man. It's "one shot, multiple kill" with the enemy of our souls. He fights dirty, so guard your marriages, men. Stand firm and keep yourself covered. And always lead from the front.

Just as in the combat theater, the leader of the family is target number one. If you happen to be active in ministry, the church or even in the arena of evangelism, you are a serious target of interest to the enemy as well. You, my friend, are a spiritual M-60. You aren't just leading your family, you're also laying down relentless harassing fire on the enemy and he's not real happy about it. Every time you open your mouth, you are sending 500 rounds of Jesus per minute over 1000 yards downrange. And whenever you pull that spiritual trigger, you make a direct impact on the kingdom of darkness, and the enemy would like nothing better than to shut you down.

Have you noticed a trend in pastors losing their churches lately? It's almost epidemic, as men are falling prey to anger issues or "moral failure," also known as "having an affair." Out of the spotlight are countless pastoral marriages fading away or lost completely, due to neglect. So many pastors spend an inordinate amount of time trying to heal busted marriages in their congregations via middle of the night counseling sessions yet ignore the same warning signals at home. And boom, the marriage goes down in a ball of flame.

Then there's the nearly impossible mission field known as "pastor's kids." I see them by the hundreds across the nation at Teen Challenge Men's Centers, which are residential drug rehabilitation homes. Over 50 percent of the guys I meet there grew up in the church and about two out of every ten are "PK's." The reason? Dad is too busy doing the work of the church to do the work at home. And another spiritual M-60, along with sometimes thousands of people at his church, is lost.

Rest assured, if you're solid in your leadership at home as a husband and father, and you're making a real impact for the Kingdom of God, you can be sure you'll receive incoming fire almost daily. You may already be there. You really are a target.

Lastly, there's the radio operator. Let me ask you a question. When life goes wrong, for whatever reason, have you ever noticed you don't want to talk to anybody? I see it in my life all the time and often say "When things go wrong, I shoot my own radio operator." Work isn't going well, we take a huge financial hit, or I'm just totally out of commission regarding my spiritual life and my best friend always seems to choose that as the perfect time to call me. I look at the screen of my phone, see his name, and immediately poke the little red "Ignore" X and dump the call to voicemail. I love the guy, but now is definitely not the time to be chatting about anything, so I don't answer. I go off the 'net' because I don't want to talk to anybody. Suddenly, I'm completely alone, which is just how I want it. I don't want to relive the nightmare-of-the-day, so I sink into the couch cushions and binge watch ESPN SportsCenter.

Then I take my communications blackout to a whole other level and I stop praying. I'm defeated and alone. I don't want to talk to my friends and I don't really even want to talk to God about it either. Ever been there?

Unfortunately, not only is alone and isolated where I'd rather be in this kind of moment, this is also exactly where the enemy wants me, too. An isolated soldier is a dead soldier. I have no covering fire, no one watching my "six" and I won't be calling in close air support when I'm "off comms." So you see, if I get hit as the leader and as the machine gunner, I cut myself off. I pretty much kill my own radio guy, so to speak. And the enemy wins.

Gentlemen, we are the primary target of any enemy offensive. Satan knows an army without command, a dead machine gunner, and no radio is an easy victory. The second we take our eyes off of this often-utilized set of tactics is the moment the enemy takes major ground in our homes.

And while we may not think we're in a theater of war, in many ways, we are. And the system in which we are fighting may also be antiquated. It's time to change the system.

So where in your own life have you felt like a downed officer? Have you met anyone lately who is clearly battle-wounded from ministry? Have you ever gone off the net just to avoid talking to your buddies? Do you remember why?

4

ON ENEMY GROUND

I want to stop here and orient you to a couple of phrases that may not be in your everyday vocabulary. We'll be using both words as we move forward, as they are key to a successful mission as a man of God. Of course, if you're military, you'll be tracking with me right away. If not, here is brief introduction.

The first phrase is "outside the wire." The wire is, well, wire. If you're a soldier at Fort Hood and you find yourself outside the wire, you are in the city of Killeen, Texas. However, should you be at Region Command South at the Kandahar Airport in Afghanistan and you happen to wander outside the wire, you are officially on hostile ground. Every forward operating base (FOB) in the theater of combat is typically surrounded by a fence line, for the obvious purpose of keeping the bad guys out.

In most circumstances, the temporary accommodations aren't exactly "home," but it's the best there is given the conditions. In Vietnam and Korea, they were mostly tents, but as we moved into OIF (Operation Iraqi Freedom) and OEF (Operation Enduring Freedom-Afghanistan), the FOB consisted mostly of trailers and plywood structures. However, the fences and gates remained a consistent feature, along with artillery batteries, guard towers, car bomb barricades and other defense systems to keep the soldiers safe.

When inside the FOB, the soldiers are as secure as they can be given where they are. But every day, patrols mount up, the gates swing open, and the convoys roll out into the battlefield. They move "outside the wire," where they are no longer in the safe confines of "home away from home," but are rather on the enemy's dirt until they return.

And when these guys head out, they are in full "battle rattle," or fighting gear. This includes body armor, helmet (these days with mounted cameras), gloves, boots, eye protection, ear protection, radio, medical kit, MRE's (food), extra magazines, a sidearm, and their rifle. Many soldiers carry far more these days, but back in the Vietnam War, a lot of guys packed light and didn't have much more than their clothes, a helmet, some food and a canteen, and their M-16.

The second phrase, or rather a term, is "downrange," In today's military, it is often a term used interchangeably with "deployed." When a soldier is downrange, that soldier isn't at home in the good old USA. The word is actually a marksmanship term. When I was twelve years old, learning to shoot a .22 rifle, the first thing my father taught me was to always keep a loaded weapon pointed downrange. You never aim a weapon at anything you aren't prepared to shoot. If you've been to a shooting range, you'll find people with firearms at one end of the range. At the other end, are the targets, which many times are human-shaped cutouts. The simplest way to describe the term "downrange" is simply this: If you are "downrange," you are on the wrong end of an operating weapon. You are the target, not the shooter.

In short, when a soldier is "outside the wire," and "downrange," he is both no longer in the safe confines of the FOB, and he is often in contact with the enemy. In Vietnam, for example, it wasn't uncommon for soldiers to be subjected to enemy fire nearly every day.

So how does this apply to regular men like us, who are just trying to survive a life filled with less life-threatening but sometimes equally debilitating life circumstances like rocky marriages, unhappy bosses, and crazy kids?

To get where I'm coming from, we need to take a look at a couple of stories from the Bible. The first story is about Satan himself, also known as the enemy. If you've ever been in Sunday School as a kid, you've likely heard the story of Adam and Eve, who were given responsibility for the Garden of Eden. They had access to the best of everything and really only had one solid rule—"Don't eat the fruit from the tree of the Knowledge of Good and Evil."

Seemingly out of nowhere, Satan came creeping up to Eve in the form of a snake, and said, "God knows that your eyes will be opened as soon as you eat it, and you will be like God," (Gen. 3:5 NLT). In spite of any potential consequences, Eve and Adam decided to eat the fruit.

The big question I've always had is "How did Satan end up in the Garden of Eden in the first place?" Conventional theological commentaries often point to the fact that Satan is actually a fallen angel, Lucifer, whose pride and desire to be on level ground with God caused him to lose his position in Heaven. He was technically the "worship leader," and got the boot from Heaven when he got prideful.

In chapter ten of the Gospel of Luke, shortly after His seventy-two disciples return from their two-by-two mission, the men excitedly tell their Master how "even demons submit to us in Your Name" (v 17). Jesus's reply points to the aforementioned fall of Lucifer when He says "I saw Satan fall like lightning from heaven," (v 18). Jesus was most likely pointing His disciples, and us, to a time in the Old Testament when the prophet Isaiah alludes to Lucifer's downfall:

How you have fallen from heaven,
morning star, son of the dawn!
You have been cast down to the earth,
you who once laid low the nations!
You said in your heart,
"I will ascend to the heavens;
I will raise my throne above the stars of God;
I will sit enthroned on the mount of assembly,
on the utmost heights of Mount Zaphon.
I will ascend above the tops of the clouds;
I will make myself like the Most High."

Isaiah 14:12–14

Now I have absolutely no idea where Mount Zaphon is but it's pretty clear God is addressing Lucifer here. And the soon-to-be fallen angel's reply is basically something along the lines of "Well, I'm going to set myself above God and make myself just like Him." Isn't it interesting the enemy recites nearly the same words to God he uses to tempt poor Eve? It's obvious trying to be like God never ends well. And it likely resulted in Lucifer's fall.

I guess the next logical question would be "So if he fell, where did he land?"

The Apostle Paul wrote something that just may be the answer in his letter to the Corinthians:

In their case the god of this world has blinded the minds of the unbelievers, to keep them from seeing the light of the gospel of the glory of Christ, who is the image of God.

2 Corinthians 4:4 ESV

Notice Paul calls Satan the "god of the world," with a lower case "g."

My conclusion, simply based upon the concept of a fallen enemy who landed somewhere, is the world we live in is devil's dirt. Sure, God has authority over him but at the end of the day, the world is the enemy's playground. And he keeps blind people from seeing the Glory of God every single day.

Finally, and most importantly, I want to look at some words of Jesus as He prays for His disciples in the Gospel of John:

I pray for them. I am not praying for the world, but for those you have given me, for they are yours. . . . My prayer is not that you take them out of the world but that you protect them from the evil one. They are not of the world, even as I am not of it.

John 17:9 and 17:15–16

Jesus clearly identifies His disciples as "not of the world," and prays protection over them from the "evil one"—Satan. He even likens them to Himself, as He is also not from the world.

As believers in Jesus, when we accept Him as our personal Lord and Savior, an amazing event happens. Essentially, we jettison our citizenship here on Earth and become adopted sons of the Most High God. It's a supernatural exchange, where we surrender our birth certificate from here. At that moment, our native homeland shifts to Heaven, where we will ultimately be for eternity. We are, like Jesus's disciples, not of the world, just as He is not. We are citizens of Heaven.

Are you ready to radically shift the paradigm of what it means to be a warrior for God?

The textbook definition of a "military deployment" is this:

Sending troops into duty. The distribution of forces to a foreign location, in preparation for battle or work, until such a time as the mission is completed, at which point the soldiers return home.

When a soldier is deployed, he is often on hostile ground, usually far from home, and is most probably facing daily contact from an enemy who has one mission—destroy that soldier and everyone around him.

Think about this. If we are indeed now citizens of Heaven, and the world is not our home, we are really on a seventy-five to ninety-five-year deployment. We are downrange, in enemy territory, and frankly on some pretty hostile ground for however long our lifetime lasts. We don't belong here permanently and as with any deployment, we will ultimately return to our homeland after the mission is over. Once our rotation here on Earth is completed, we will leave the battlefield and head home to Heaven.

Knowing this, we would likely be far better off if we realized each morning, when we walk out our front door, we are really rolling outside the wire. We are embarking on our daily mission into the world and there will most definitely be hostile contact from our enemy. The only question is, will we survive? If you leave the FOB without your gear, the answer is probably going to be "No." Sure, we may not get taken out today but without body armor, weapons, and covering fire, it's a gamble, and there's a good chance the enemy will get a lucky shot off eventually.

To be prepared, we need to give heed to Paul's words to the Ephesians:

Therefore put on the full armor of God, so that when the day of evil comes, you may be able to stand your ground, and after you have done everything, to stand. Stand firm then, with the belt of truth buckled around your waist, with the breastplate of righteousness in place, and with your feet fitted with the readiness that comes from the gospel of peace. In addition to all this, take up the shield of faith, with which you can extinguish all the flaming arrows of the evil one. Take the helmet of salvation and the sword of the Spirit, which is the word of God.

Ephesians 6:13–17

You can change the words up to make those verses more technically contemporary, like "the body armor of righteousness in place," "the helmet-cam of salvation," and the "M-4 of the Spirit," if you prefer. The premise doesn't change, whether we're talking about a desert-era combat soldier or a 1st Century Roman centurion.

We suit up before we roll. We recognize we're in enemy territory all day, every day. And we must fight as a team, not as a solo operator.

Have you ever rolled out of home base without your armor on? Did you think of life as a combat theater? What will you do differently, tactically, now that you are situationally aware of your surroundings?

5

IT'S ALL ABOUT THE FIRETEAM

S ervice. It's a word us church guys are all too familiar with. We can only sit in the backrow and duck out unnoticed for so long before we begin to feel the Holy Spirit-led pull to get involved. Join a small group, work as an usher, join the worship team—just do something to "get plugged in."

My introduction to service was more like a draft than the intentional act of a volunteer. The Holy Spirit led my wife to the worship team and the worship leader consequently discovered I play drums (something I'd kept well-hidden as a veteran of sitting in the back pew). Needless to say, they were missing a drummer on an upcoming weekend and the worship leader literally chased us down in the parking lot to recruit me, in spite of having never heard me play a single beat.

After that random weekend as a fill-in drummer, I found myself behind the kit in front of a few thousand people every Sunday. I didn't resign my drum throne until the speaking side of Rough Cut Men got so busy I had to put my sticks back in my gear bag permanently. During my tenure as part of the rhythm section, I made a lot of friends. Ushers, greeters, singers, and pre-service prayer guys were my circle of buddies since we were together so often.

But being mostly men, our relationship pretty much stopped after the service was over. Our conversations were usually about an inch deep and revolved around the Florida Gators or the latest music downloads.

After departing the band years earlier and subsequently moving to a new church, one of the guys from the old church called me on the phone to tell me one of his close family members was dying of cancer and had only weeks to live. I was surprised to get the call, because I assumed he must have had better friends than me. Honestly, we barely knew each other at all, other than passing on Sunday, and exchanging the compulsory high five or fist bump.

We met for coffee and I told him I was always available to yell at, punch, and cry all over—I was a safe place to let his guard down and just deal with the emotions that had to remain concealed while being the "big and bad, and in control" dad and husband. He took me up on it and we talked several times after that, ultimately both fading back into our disconnected life as usual.

After several months of dead air, my phone again lit up with missed calls from the same guy. I knew it was urgent and my fear was his relative passed and I wasn't there to catch him when he fell. "I need to talk to you," he said. "Can you meet me at the library?" My first thought was, *What guy wants to meet at a library?* but I obliged. As I pulled into the parking lot, there he was. He started walking toward my car, visibly shaken. By the time he arrived at the passenger door, he broke down like a little kid who hurt himself on the playground but didn't want to cry until he saw his mom. He proceeded to inform me, while inadvertently sitting next to his wife's phone, he read several very inappropriate texts from another guy.

Recounting a tale of marriage counseling, a complete melt-down, and numerous X-rated texts from this "other guy," my buddy simply concluded his tale by asking for a ride to meet his wife and a counseling couple. I dropped him off, only to again get called within two minutes to pick him up. This time, he wasn't sobbing but red-faced and furious. "She's pregnant," he yelled at me from about eighteen inches away, "and it's not mine"!

Now, I'm a man whose friend has just been cheated on. My first instinct was to track this other dude down and make him pay. My friend knew who the other guy was so zeroing in on the perpetrator would be easy. Maybe a throat punch or throw a "blanket party" (you can Google that one if you've never heard the term) would be a solid consequence? But my friend adamantly refused retribution of any kind.

At night, I would contemplate this man's seemingly no-win scenario. *How can he have this child*, I thought to myself, *because every time he sees that kid, he'll be reminded of this horrible time in his life.* At one point, I even mentioned leaving to him and I could see him wrestling with the option of just walking away. Then, seemingly out of nowhere, God changed my heart to align with both my friend's, and His.

I was reminded of how my kids didn't meet the Lord until after their mother and I split up and I met God as well. And how, being a part time dad for years adversely impacted my kids. It was clear this little baby, whose biological dad was out of the picture, would be far better off in a Christian home. So my friend stayed, had the baby with his wife, and both accepted their new son as their own. And God won a huge victory that day, both in their home and in my heart.

My point in sharing this story is to pose a question: "Why was I the only guy in his life he could call?" After all, we're "church guys," surrounded by dozens of other like-minded men who meet every Sunday by the hundreds, even thousands. The answer is really simple. We just don't know anyone. Sure, we know names but that's where it ends. And it really wasn't until I started working with combat soldiers of all generations that I realized where we're going wrong as a Kingdom army.

Have you ever watched any of those predator shows? No, not the Arnold-meets-the-alien *Predator* movies, the actual predator documentaries you see on the National Geographic channel. On the screen, we often witness a pack of wolves or a pride of lions graphically dismember some unsuspecting gazelle or hapless goat? The last time I watched a program like that, I noticed predators are often pack hunters, and they systemically separate one of the herd out to take it down. In this particular episode, the victim was a gazelle who'd simply wandered down to a stream alone to get a quick drink, only to be overwhelmed by a dozen lions. The part that was so interesting was the size of the prey. He wasn't some weak little gazelle but a really big one. My takeaway from the attack was this: The enemy doesn't necessarily go after the weak one. He goes after the one who's dumb enough to be going solo.

The more time I spend with soldiers, the more I realize how completely upside-down our concept of supporting men in the church really is. Honestly, we're doing it all backward. To add insult to injury, it's becoming increasingly evident our enemy—the same one who comes to "steal, kill and destroy"—operates an awful lot like a true military combatant. And we, as God's army, truly don't give the enemy the credit he deserves for being effective in isolating soldiers and picking off leaders.

To best understand the inherent infrastructure of any successful group, let's look at our very own United States Army:

Organizationally, from the top down, the U.S. Army consists of around 475,000 active duty soldiers in Field Armies, each consisting of somewhere between two and five "Corps." As of today, there are actually only three Corps—I Corps is at

Joint Base Lewis-McChord near Tacoma, Washington, III Corps is located at Fort Hood in Killeen, Texas, and the XVIII Airborne Corps, headquartered at Fort Bragg in Fayetteville, North Carolina. Each Corps consists of two to five "Divisions" of between ten-eighteen thousand soldiers each.

Divisions are legendary and are usually the units they make movies about. *We Were Soldiers*, for example, depicts the 1st Cavalry Division. Do you recall the epic war movie *The Big Red One*, starring Lee Marvin? That was the 1st Infantry Division. And if you've ever seen *Saving Private Ryan* or watched the miniseries *Band of Brothers*, you've witnessed the World War II heroism of the 101st Airborne Division.

Continuing with our breakdown of the Army, each Division is comprised of three or more "Brigades" of roughly three to five thousand men each. Brigades are broken down into three or more "Battalions" (or Squadrons) of 300–1300 soldiers, who are each reduced into smaller 100 to 200-man elements called "Companies," Companies are broken into "Platoons" of around fifteen to thirty soldiers, then into Squads of around eight to twelve, and finally, the fireteam of four. Notice how we went from over a half million soldiers in the Army down to four people?

A standard four-man fireteam consists of a team leader, a rifleman, a grenadier, and an automatic weapons guy (a SAW gunner, or Squad Automatic Weapon). In other words, you have a man on point who directs the action, a guy who can target specific enemy assets with a rifle, another man who can level the trees with grenades and the machine gunner, who can lay down covering fire at a really high cyclic rate.

When the fireteam is downrange and rolls outside the wire, they are on their own. There's a guy driving, another riding shotgun next to him (usually the team leader), another man in the back seat and finally, another soldier with his head sticking through a hole in the roof, manning the 50-caliber machine gun turret. Sure, they have a fire support guy out there somewhere, who can call in artillery, and close air support if they need it but they are otherwise on mission as a four-man team.

Each man typically has a different weapon, but they all have each other's "six," or back. They have a mission to execute, which is actually more like two missions in one. The first mission is to accomplish whatever task they've been ordered to carry out but the second and more important mission, is they all make it back to the Forward Operating Base or "FOB," together. Dead or alive, they're all coming back.

Recently, I had the privilege of attending a high-level Change of Command ceremony at Joint Base Lewis-McChord for a great friend of mine who was taking over a Stryker Brigade. The change of command ceremony is an iconic ritual, where the Guidon (their unit flag) is passed from the outgoing commander and his sergeant major, to the incoming commander and sergeant major. It's a celebration, where soldiers are in their Class A uniforms, families attend, the band is playing, and cannons are fired. At the conclusion of this particular ceremony, the entire Brigade paraded past my friend, saluting him unit by unit, accompanied by the band, in a "Pass-and-Review." It was an incredible sight to witness.

During the ceremony, I was reminded of another one I attended, where I encountered a battalion of soldiers who were set to deploy to Afghanistan almost immediately upon the conclusion of the celebration. They were dismissed, only to return to their barracks to don their ACU's, grab their gear, and head downrange. In the span of a day, they went from shiny shoes and marching bands, to dirty ACU's, hard cots, and "weapons hot."

Once downrange, any brigade gatherings are long forgotten when in close contact with the enemy. What's happening at Division HQ, or even at home, is no longer important. Their Class A dress uniforms are probably in a hanging bag in a closet back home and they are in the fight. Each man looks out for his brothers until they come home. Why? Because they spend time together, fighting for each other. And most importantly, they trust each other. At that moment, they don't care about anything but the team.

Like it or not, the battle, and often the war, is won or lost at the fireteam level. Period. Each man comes into the team with different skills and weaponry and they each execute their respective responsibilities. If the team is missing one element of the fireteam, the menu of tactics has to change to accommodate his absence. In many cases, the handicap of a missing man can be crippling.

Now take a look at the way we "do" church as men. When we get men together for a men's event or a Sunday morning service (or in this case, a Brigade or Division parade, where everyone looks sharp), it should be to regale each other with stories from the battlefield. We'll never build solid friendships while on that "parade ground" we call a "men's conference" for a weekend. If our goal is to create friendships while warming a pew, we've missed the mark. I was in a band with a dozen guys and we never talked about anything other than chord progressions and our favorite football teams. It wasn't until my friend was in the fight of his relational life that we broke through the "stranger barrier" and truly started watching out for each other.

I can assure you that piling 80,000 men into a stadium for a conference likely won't create battle-ready relationships, any more than parading an entire brigade in Class A dress uniforms through the jungle would. If the Army decided to assemble a Division on the parade ground and then somehow hoped teams would form after the assembly, it would be an epic military fail. The crucible of battle forges unbreakable relationships.

These relationships don't just happen instantly. They are constructed over time and often in the context of extreme duress. On the first day of a nine-month deployment, it's not uncommon for the soldiers inside a Humvee to be relative strangers, in spite of being in the same unit. The conversations usually revolve around where the guys are from, how many kids they have, how long they've been in the Army and who they root for on game day. But as time passes, the conversations get real. Instead of football, one of the team mentions he's afraid his wife is cheating on him while he's downrange or a child is sick and he can't be there for his family. Time, coupled with relentless enemy contact, drive men into deeper brotherhood.

I failed to mention one of the more important components of the fireteam which has morphed through the last century of warfare. In the earlier wars, alongside every squad or platoon of warfighters was a medic, often nicknamed, "The Doc". The Doc had the medical supplies to triage the wounded in the field and to give them the life-sustaining care needed until the wounded soldier could be evacuated from the battlefield to get more specialized medical treatment.

Over time, however, it became clear there was an inherent problem with the medic concept. If a soldier was wounded, one of his buddies would immediately yell for a medic. Often, that medic was either out of earshot or couldn't hear over the sounds of the battlefield. Worse yet, the medic may have been on the far side of an impassable landing zone with no way to get to the injured. In either case, the wounded would die while waiting for help.

In more modern times, especially the recent desert warfare era, a simple adjustment was made. Nearly every soldier fighting now has a med kit or at minimum, someone in the team has one. They have the ability to plug wounds, give morphine, and execute tasks to ensure a fair shot at survival while either waiting for the "Doc" or a helicopter to get their wounded teammate off the field. Consequently, the survival rate of downrange wounded has increased significantly since the implementation of a med guy in a fireteam.

We can apply this same line of thinking to how we deal with wounded brothers in life. We should be able to "relationally triage" our own wounded without delay. When my friend opened my car door, crying and devastated, the last thing I thought of doing was running him to the church or over to the pastor's house. After all, I'm qualified to walk this guy though the valley without a degree in theology. He just needed a brother to lean on and I was there. There's a really good chance he would have never stood up at a men's conference and shouted, "My wife cheated on me and now she's pregnant." That was between him and me. There was trust and he knew I had his "six."

My personal mission as a ministry to the Army is similar in that we are training soldiers to care for each other when "life happens," without having to drag the guy to a Chaplain. Men need other men and the battles are fought at the fireteam level of friendship. You know you don't have to know what it's like to lose a marriage, lose a spouse or lose a house to be there for another man. It's in times like this when men don't need someone to wax poetic about Scripture or preach at them. They just need a friend.

Men, we need fireteams. If we are indeed "outside the wire" when we get up in the morning, we'd be fools to head out solo. We need covering fire, we need someone watching our backs and we need friends. Let me suggest something.

If you're a part of church, go find two or three other guys and just spend time together. Don't wait for "Headquarters" to do it at some random Saturday men's breakfast. Link up this week! We only trust other men when we spend time together and as long as we don't get burned. Trust only happens when I know you have my back and you know I have yours.

Ask any combat vet how he feels about his team. They'd die for each other. Long after the war is over, that bond of friendship is rock solid.

It's time to get off the parade ground and get into the fight. The war is always raging at our doorstep and we don't need any more casualties.

Do you have "that guy" in your life? The one who will pick up when you call at 2 AM or meet you in the parking lot of a library when life blows up? Or are you in the firefight of your life right now, with no overwatch?

Now that we know we are in a war and the critical nature of having a team of men on our "six," we need to understand exactly who this enemy is we're all dealing with. We also need to zero in on how the successes in the Ia Drang Valley over fifty years ago, at every rank, relate to how we battle for our families, marriages, and kids today.

KNOW YOUR ENEMY AND YOUR RESOURCES

Y ou can see the pressure and the anticipation play out in the movie. Deploying in mere weeks, Hal Moore, the commander of "Garryowen" sits at his desk at home, staring at images from the massacre of the French Army which occurred eleven years earlier in an area known as "An Khe." The French previously encountered the same devastating guerilla tactics of the Vietnamese at both Dien Bien Phu in 1954 and Cao Bang in 1950. So Moore had a pretty good idea of what he would be up against.

The prevailing word is "ambush," which ironically led to the downfall of Moore's 7th Cavalry predecessor, General George Armstrong Custer, at Little Big Horn. My wife and I always say, "Once is coincidence, twice is a trend." It is clear the 1st Battalion of the 7th Cavalry was likely walking into a similar scenario and preparation would be the linchpin to success on the battlefield.

In an effort to be battle-ready, Moore took it upon himself to not only study his enemy but also his mission capabilities. After all, his newly-formed unit was "beta-testing" several completely new concepts in warfare, starting with the implementation of helicopters to facilitate troop movements. Second, his men would be carrying the brand-new M-16 rifle into combat for the first time. And to top it all off, the battleground was nearly 14,000 miles away from home.

The consummate tactician, Moore studied the terrain specific to the Central Highlands of South Vietnam, an area peppered with huge anthills, dense jungles, and vegetation such as Elephant Grass, which could cut like a razor and conceal the enemy like a green curtain. Some of the guys who fought in the Ia Drang Valley shared stories of that Elephant Grass, stating the enemy could be just on the other side of it and they could neither be heard nor seen. Five feet on the other side of a weed and our guys didn't even know the enemy was there.

Not unaware of this new enemy's penchant for ambush, Moore became familiar with their battle tactics as it related to their "home terrain." In essence, he knew what to expect before the first shot was fired. He knew what the enemy would be hiding behind, what weapons they'd be firing at him, and where they'd likely be coming from. Sun Tzu, in *The Art of War* wrote "to defeat your enemy, you have to know your enemy." And Moore knew his enemy.

And then there was the Bell UH-1 Iroquois helicopter, which was the present-day equivalent to Custer's horse. Nicknamed the "Huey," this machine would be their lifeline between the battlefield and the Forward Operating Base. Some would transport troops to the field, others would carry ARA (Aerial Rocket Artillery), while others would be DUSTOFF (an acronym for 'Dedicated Unhesitating Service To Our Fighting Forces') or MEDEVAC (Medical Evacuation) helicopters.

Moore became a student of the Huey, mastering both its capabilities and its limitations. He knew the top air speed, maximum altitude, and number of men in full "battle rattle" potentially carried by each bird. Moore also knew the total flight time between the FOB to the Area of Operations, which was roughly a thirty minute round trip. The Commander of the 1/7 CAV knew his tools, his support, and who he was up against. As men of God, it's no secret who our enemy is. You've heard all the names—Satan, the devil, Beelzebub, Lucifer, etc.—right?. Famous Dutch watchmaker and theologian, Corrie Ten Boom, whose family successfully concealed countless Jews during the Holocaust, wrote, "The first step on the way to victory is to recognize the enemy."

The apostle Peter gives us a really solid, non-sugar-coated description of who we're fighting:

"Be alert and of sober mind. Your enemy the devil prowls around like a roaring lion looking for someone to devour"

—1 Peter 5:8

I'm not a fan of lions. We live near a place called "Big Cat Habitat," which is essentially a hospital for sick or injured feline predators. On a quiet morning, we can hear them roaring, in spite of the over-four-mile distance between us. They scare me to death, even when they're behind a huge wall at the zoo. Remember the plight of the thirsty gazelle from the last chapter?

Guys, we have an enemy who wants to kill us. He wants us dead. Out of the picture. Gone. That is his primary missional objective. Actually, it's really his only objective. Take the man out of the family, the family goes down.

Like Hal Moore, we should be perpetually training for the impending battle. Honestly, since we already know the motivation of our enemy, there should really never be a surprise attack.

Paul is pretty clear about our Spiritual "situational awareness" in 2 Corinthians 2:11:

"in order that Satan might not outwit us. For we are not unaware of his schemes."

Come on, guys. We're no dummies, right? We already know our weak spots. Most of the time, we know precisely where the enemy will drop the bomb, even before he opens the bomb bay door.

Since I'm no stranger to an almost-constant barrage of enemy fire in life, I thought I'd pass on a great tip to survive those days when the devil is all over you. If you want to stay ahead of the enemy, think like him.

Wait, what? No, really. Think like the enemy. When you get up in the morning, ask yourself, "What would I do to totally throw myself off today?" or "If I really wanted to ruin my day, what would I hit hard?" Then proactively pray against it.

Dave Moore is Hal Moore's youngest son of their five children. Dave, like his father, is a graduate of West Point and a retired Army officer who served in the combat theater during Desert Storm. During one of our conversations, as Dave was recounting his time at Infantry Officer Basic, he stopped to share an interesting vignette about his dad. "I don't mean to sound crazy, but I swear my dad can predict the future," he said, "Not like a fortune teller, but he can anticipate outcomes like no one I know. He is always circumstantially aware and can plan future actions based on the current situation."

Joe Galloway, who reported every second of the three-day battle from the field and often found himself next to Hal Moore under enemy fire, said almost the same thing about his best friend. Moore's ability to predict the opposition force's movements is portrayed vividly in *We Were Soldiers*, when Moore masses reinforcements at the precise location where the North Vietnamese were preparing to hit the hardest. And when asked how he knew where the bad guys were going to attack, Moore simply responds with, "Well, that's what I would've done." One of the most polished battle leaders in Army history often succeeded in battle by thinking like the enemy. We, too, should be aware of where the enemy will hit us, long before he starts "testing the fences."

In my own life, for example, I'm acutely aware the enemy will use my adult kids against me. If he succeeds in getting me worked up enough about them, I take my eyes off the mission to focus on the problem. A few years ago, I was standing on the platform at the West Point Club at the United States Military Academy, seconds away from addressing a group of cadets. I frequently set my phone on the podium next to my speaker notes in order to keep track of time and this day was no different. As I inhaled one last time before going live, my phone vibrated.

It was one brief, two-word text message from my son: "I'm homeless." The words glared at me, crushing my gut. As a father, you never want your children to be in a situation like this. It's not like it came as a surprise. He moved out two days before his eighteenth birthday and subsequently lived in three different states with at least a half dozen different people. Clearly, he was officially out of options but the timing of the message was just too tactically perfect. My thoughts raced, "Now? You choose to tell me this now? I'm setting up for one of the biggest events in the history of our ministry and this is what I get?"

It wasn't until these sorts of texts became a trend I concluded the enemy was using these perfectly timed attacks to distract me from the mission at hand. After all, if I'm off my game, the message loses impact. I usually only get one shot at speaking to a particular group of people and the enemy knows it. So, in an effort to launch a spiritual counter-offensive, I now do one thing religiously prior to speaking. I turn my phone off. Sure, I let my wife know and I make certain there's a way to begin and end on time but I go "off the net." Believe it or not, I haven't missed a single catastrophe. Life goes on. And the mission also goes on—uncompromised.

Galloway once told me Moore had the ability to disengage from the battlefield action for thirty to sixty seconds to ask himself two simple questions. Bullets could be whizzing past his head with artillery exploding just yards away and Moore would stop dead in his tracks to evaluate the situation using two benchmarks:

1. What I am doing right now that I shouldn't be doing?
2. What should I be doing right now that I'm not doing?

You know, just pulling the plug long enough to think clearly, without reacting out of fear, anger or just plain knee-jerking, is always a great way to tip the cards back in our favor. Are we doing something in our lives to compromise the mission? Are we missing clear direction from God while pinned down in "reactive mode"? It's amazing how many times I get in a jam at home when I speak before I think, so now I stop long enough to ask myself if what I'm about to say is positive or just antagonistic. It works, trust me. Don't return fire until you know what the shot is. Or don't fire at all.

Here are some fail safe and battle tested methods for victory over the enemy:

1. *Anticipate Challenges:* Just like my text messaging tactic, know the weak spots in your line and reinforce them accordingly. Survival starts with situational awareness.
2. *Be Proactive, Not Reactive:* Pray in the morning against the very thing or person, who will throw your actions for the day into confusion or anger. I find praying for my greatest antagonist often blesses me in the process. At the very least, I rescind permission for them to rob my joy, which is all I have on some days.
3. *Know your "Choke Points".* A military choke point is defined as *a geographical feature such as a valley or a bridge, which an armed force is forced to pass, sometimes on a substantially*

narrower front, and therefore greatly decreasing its combat power. A choke point can allow a numerically inferior defending force to successfully thwart a larger opponent if the attacker cannot bring superior numbers to bear. In more recent eras, like Iraq, a choke point could be a city street. Let's say you turn down a narrow city alley with a two-story building on either side. At the end is a big truck parked across the alley. Here's a tip: Don't turn down that alley. It's a choke point and you're probably going to get heavy contact from an elevated position. They're going to shoot at you from the roofline or from behind the truck. Worse yet, they may block you in with another truck. Then you're in the "kill box," with the enemy in the superior overhead position and you with no way out.

In our lives, we must be aware of our own choke points. You've heard people say, "If you're an alcoholic, stay out of the bar." Makes sense, right? If you have a weak point, don't go there. The enemy wants you to click on that link on your computer. He wants you to buy that thing you can't afford or end up fired because you popped off to your boss. If he gets you to take the bait, to turn down that alley, he's got you. The trick is to recognize it for what it is—a way to take you out of the mission. A man battling his wife over a pornography addiction is no longer focused on the directives of Godly manhood or parenting. And an isolated and paralyzed soldier is usually mere moments away from being a dead soldier.

4. *Be Aware of Battle Lines.* This is one I often lose sight of in the "fog of war" known as my life. I work so hard to execute my disciplines, like spending time reading the Word, praying for my family, and you'd have to look pretty hard to find someone who works harder or expends longer hours on the Kingdom job. But I tend to forget my role as a leader in my

family and if I look the other way for too long, suddenly my marriage is getting hammered. And when that's going well, my kids can arbitrarily drift off the mark. Here's the deal. The enemy will stop at nothing to get you to look the other way. If you have eyes on target, someone in your ranks on the perimeter may be the likely next target. Face it, if our marriage is rough, or the kids are off the rails, we end up focusing our energy on damage control instead of moving forward. It's win/win for the enemy. Either he hits us directly, or he goes after a weaker link on our team.

During the Battle of Ia Drang and in subsequent months in the same area of operations, the enemy soldiers repeatedly relied on ambush. A quarter-mile long column of American soldiers makes for an easy target. Regardless who the enemy selected to shoot, the entire column would stop. Whether it was a seasoned field commander or an eighteen-year-old draftee, when a man went down, no further forward progress happened until the ambush was over and the wounded received the first aid they needed. In other words, even if your life is hitting on all cylinders, your kids can be easy targets. And the whole column, known as our family unit, is off-mission until the problem is handled.

There are no rules with the devil and he fights dirty. Don't lose awareness of the position of the others on your team. They're on your watch, too.

In a nutshell, the trick to surviving these types of relentless, aptly timed attacks is to be aware they're coming. Pray against them before the enemy gets off a shot. What about you? What one thing could the devil throw at you that would ruin the day? Which choke point could result in a "one shot/multiple kill" scenario by the enemy? For some of us, our own worst enemy is the guy who stares back at us every morning in the bathroom mirror and that interaction sets the tone for the entire day. Where has the enemy taken the liberty of pinning you down?

CHAPTER

7

LET THE PAST GO

E very day during the Vietnam War, including over the three days Moore's 1/7 CAV unit was in the Ia Drang valley, a lot of good men died. From November 14–16, 1965, seventy-nine U.S. Troopers were killed in action, and 121 were wounded, making it the highest toll to date in the escalating Vietnam conflict. That's seventy-nine men over three days who never made it home and over 120 additional men who were out of the fight. You can be sure those deaths impacted the men who were fortunate enough to live another day or more appropriately, fight another day.

If you've ever lost someone close to you, it's debilitating. And, not just for a few days, as something is altered every subsequent day we outlive the person who didn't make it. Unfortunately, my wife lost her father in 1989 and her mother in 2008, and it's not uncommon to find her quietly crying on holidays. Stupid me, I always forget her parents are both gone, so in typical guy style I ask, "What's wrong?" "I miss my parents," she sobs. It's been over ten years now since her mother passed, and over twenty-five since she lost her father but the wound is there, and it's real.

Now translate that same pain of loss to the battlefield, where men lose their best friends to enemy fire. In the Ia Drang Valley, the second day saw ferocious fighting and massive loss of life on both sides. As a soldier, how could you fight the next day, after watching your buddies fall to your right and to your left? I will never forget Joe Galloway's tearful recount of a moment in the Ia Drang Valley where he had to duck to avoid a flying arm blown off of the man he was running behind as they charged toward the enemy. I can sometimes barely get out of bed when things aren't going well with my kids or my wife but the emotional trauma on the battlefield is unparalleled in magnitude. The pain and emotional paralysis, suffered down-range in that South Vietnamese valley must have been crushing.

In the midst of catastrophe, we sometimes completely lose our minds. No one has to die beside us to throw us into complete emotional or relational vapor lock. I failed to mention some of the events that occurred in the middle of my friend's crisis with his wife. One time in particular that really sticks out in my mind was a phone call I received while driving to an airport in North Carolina. It was my wife. "We don't know where he is," she said. My wife happened to be with my buddy's pregnant wife and he went off the grid.

When I called his cell phone, he catatonically told me he was in a parking lot at "some mall," which I determined was about fifty miles from his home. He had no idea how he got there. "I can't do this, dude," he cried. "I've made a commitment and I don't think I can go through with it." Over the span of about an hour, I managed to talk him off the ledge and he drove home. It was a near miss but he got back into the game. If you're in one of those life altering circumstances right now, you need to know you're going to make it.

When a soldier gets killed in action in the middle of a battle, I'm sure his teammates are devastated. But they don't have time to mourn, worry about it, cry over the loss, or frankly even stop moving forward. There's a time and a place for grief but in a gun fight isn't that time. In the movie *Lone Survivor,* four men from SEAL Team 10 on a recon mission in Afghanistan are discovered, and subsequently attacked by a much larger enemy Taliban force. One teammate, Danny Dietz, has already been killed, the three remaining men have been shot multiple times, and have somehow survived not one, but two violent falls down an Afghan mountainside.

Pinned down and refusing to lose, the SEALs fight relentlessly. The original mission was to locate a Taliban kingpin and call in the attack. But the mission quickly transitioned into one of mere survival. At this point, the only mission is getting the rest of the team out alive. They were outgunned and outmanned, simultaneously facing over 100 enemy combatants as a four-man team. Team leader Lt. Michael Murphy, who by now is near death himself, decides to climb to a high point to attempt to regain lost communications with their Quick Reaction Force nearby. Before climbing the hill, he hands his extra magazines over to his teammate, Marcus Luttrell, and says one line I repeat to myself every day: "Never out of the fight."

Even though a teammate goes down, the fight rages on. It may not seem like you're going to make it right now, but I can assure you, you will. I often tell men, "God didn't lead you into the desert to die."

What happened yesterday is over. What happened this morning is history. You have no choice but to get back into the fight because others are counting you. There are men around you, ready to step into the battle with you, but you have to let it go. God says the same thing in His words to Isaiah:

Forget the former things; do not dwell on the past. See, I am doing a new thing!

Isaiah 43:18

What's holding you down? Why won't you get back up and fight?

8

NEVER PAY ATTENTION TO THE ODDS

G rowing up in the Deep South, I'm all too familiar with fire ants. I spent a number of years in the Pacific Northwest, so I know there are portions of the United States that have never seen these little red monsters. In Florida, they tend to set up very large mounds, and if you step on one, literally thousands of ants come from everywhere to repair the footprint damage. They're ferociously territorial and when they bite you, not only does it hurt like crazy, but the bite gets worse over subsequent days. In fact, I've even been told the human body becomes increasingly sensitive to their venom each time one gets bitten, and I've had lots of firsthand experience as a target of their defenses.

I recall one particular fishing outing with my best friend. We grew up just a mile apart and we'd bike to each other's houses nearly every day. Of course, this was back in the day when our mothers sent us to the store on our bicycles for a gallon of milk, without fear of abduction. We rode everywhere. In our neighborhood, there were lots of little lakes surrounded by concretes walls, where we spent our weekends hunting the elusive largemouth bass. This particular Saturday was no different than any other and we were lakeside right after breakfast.

As I was casting my plastic worm, twelve-year-old me failed to notice I was standing directly in the middle of one of the fire ant mounds we were well-trained to avoid. Unaware of their underground "troop" movements, my entire leg was completely covered in ants. But these little guys are smart and bite on some sort of sadistic, synchronized signal. They move into position, patiently waiting for their silent order to chomp down on their unsuspecting victim.

All at once, my leg was on fire. I let out a scream and jumped into the water to get them off. That's when I discovered the whole "When you have ants on you, jump in the water and they'll fall off" trick was nothing more than an old wives' tale. Needless to say, my fishing day was over. And my leg was killing me.

When Hal Moore moved his battalion to the foot of the Chu Pong Massif in the Ia Drang Valley, the orders were simple: Find the enemy and kill them. Just days earlier, the North Vietnamese Army attacked one of the U.S. bases but no one was killed; the enemy just ran off into the hills. As was the fate of General Custer, Moore prepared his 395-man team for a potential ambush.

Much like a fire ant hill, Moore and his team were unaware that, directly under the mountain adjacent to the battlefield, there was an intricate network of enemy tunnels. The concealed exits from these tunnels littered the battlefield and were occupied by no fewer than 1600 enemy soldiers. In simple math, they were outnumbered five to one, which never bodes well for the smaller group. To make matters worse, when the fighting started, the enemy seemed to appear from everywhere, making them that much harder to fight. Just like those little ants, the PAVN army would establish firing positions before our guys even knew where they were.

I would be remiss if I didn't bring up one feature of the Vietnam-era U.S. Army we tend to overlook. This wasn't an all-volunteer force like we have fighting today; these guys were drafted. When a teenager hit his eighteenth birthday, more often than not, he would receive a draft card with a number. The results of the "draft lottery" were often televised, so the potential draftee and his entire family became aware of his fate over the national airwaves. And when his number was called, the draftee was given a "report date," and he officially became a soldier for a period of two years, like it or not.

Will Parish was one of those guys. He hails from Oklahoma and his DD214 (his discharge papers) state he served two years and four days in the Army. Parish is back in Oklahoma now, has raised a family of girls and after the war, just went back to life as it was before he left. In my opinion and in the opinion of many, Will Parish is a war hero. He was inducted into the Oklahoma Military Hall of Fame and even has a street named after him in his hometown of Bristow—which his daughter tells me he insists on driving her down every time she's in town to visit.

A Specialist Fourth Class, Will was a machine gunner with Charlie Company, 1st Battalion, 7th Cavalry. Charlie Company, under the command of Captain Bob Edwards, was a Heavy Weapons Infantry unit. After Basic Training at Fort Polk, Will was with the 2nd Battalion 23rd Infantry, which was ultimately joined with the 11th Air Assault. As I mentioned earlier, the 11th Air Assault we redesignated the 1st Battalion of the 7th Cavalry. And the rest is history.

In spite of not really wanting to be in the Army in the first place, Parish found himself aboard a Huey aimed for Landing Zone X-Ray. The reason his discharge papers cite he was in for four days beyond the required two years is because of this battle; He only had fourteen days left when those helicopter skids flared into the Ia Drang Valley. And once SP4 Parish was on the ground in battle, he did his job unwaveringly, just like his teammates.

As the battle was winding down, Parish and his ammo man were on the perimeter, facing an adjacent tree line. Their mission was to prevent the enemy from re-entering the wide open LZ. It was dark after Will deployed a series of trip flares wired along the tree line to warn of any unwanted enemy advances. Everything was just fine, until those little flares started to shatter the darkness, one after the other. And Will Parish started firing.

He'll tell you he doesn't remember a thing that happened after the first shell ejected from the side port of his M-60 but Parish has a solid recollection of a couple of very lucid thoughts during the enemy's hour-long attack. "I don't even know these guys and they're trying to kill me," was his first thought, followed closely by, "Are they ever gonna run out of people?" Through it all, the machinegunner just kept shooting toward the tree line.

At sunrise, it became evident what Specialist Parish did. Surrounding his shallow foxhole on a remote edge of LZ X-Ray lay over 100 dead enemy soldiers. After the action and his subsequent discharge, Parish's squad leader offered to submit him for a Silver Star but Parish states he didn't care. He will tell you, "I was only concerned about the 100-meter area around my foxhole and the man with me. I just did what I was trained to do."

In life, we will always run into those people who I call "Johnny Raincloud." These are the folks who will rattle off statistics about how people in the same situation in which we find ourselves, never made it. There will always be "naysayers," who don't think you can make it either. The odds are too great, they'll say. I've often seen it with people who have cancer, surrounded by statisticians who cavalierly tell the person in question the odds of survival. I've seen the same types of actions with friends contemplating bankruptcy or good friends whose children are battling addiction. In my own life, several different men, whom I respected as mentors, informed me I'd never survive in ministry without a book, or a "nest egg" to fund said ministry. But these people often forget one key Scripture:

Greater is he who is in you than he who is in the world

—1 John 4:4

There will always be "that guy" who'll say you aren't going to survive the battle. There will always be "white noise" around us, drowning out that "still small voice" who is the Lord. But remember, God never calls the equipped; He equips the called.

I live in Southwest Florida, the lightning capital of the United States. We used to be the "Lightning Capital of the World" until some little village in Venezuela stole the title. We're right along the western edge of Florida, near the Gulf of Mexico and unlike most parts of the country, our storms can come from both directions. In fact, sometimes our storms roll east to west, and then arbitrarily reverse direction so you get hit twice by the same storm.

In Florida, we're proud of our 1.45 million lightning strikes per year, which equates roughly twenty-five strikes per square mile. Growing up in the state, there are rules about lightning one learns in school. For example, every second you count between the flash of the lightning and the boom of the thunder represents roughly, and rather unscientifically, about a mile. After a certain distance, you can no longer even hear the thunder, but you can see the flash of lightning for nearly 100 miles. The rule is, if you can hear the thunder, get out of the pool or off the golf course. Lightning can kill you.

But lightning over 100 miles away will put out a big flash and then nothing. It makes no noise. And it can't hurt you, because it's too far away. It's just lightning out in the middle of the Gulf. The same thing holds true to all the white noise in our lives. The collections guy calling at 8:15 in the morning may throw you off, but he can't hurt you. He can take you out of your quiet time regimen with the Lord but it's just a collections call. People who say you'll never make it through something are certainly entitled to their opinion but the only thing that matters is what God says about the circumstances. The rest is just noise.

What must have the troopers of the 1/7 CAV been thinking when they realized they just landed on top of a Vietnamese ant hill? Or when they figured out they were vastly outnumbered? My guess is no one called the helicopters back, because the men from Garryowen fought like angry hornets. Not for a medal, or a news headline, but for each other. That's what we need to do as we engage our own enemy.

You may be wondering what Specialist Fourth Class Will Parish from Oklahoma was thinking when those trip flares first started popping. Truth is, he didn't take any time to think. He just stood his post. And when I asked him how he accomplished what he did, he said only one thing:

I just kept firing until the enemy stopped coming.

Have you ever found yourself in a situation where everyone around says you won't make it? Worse yet, are you telling yourself the same thing? We can all Google statistics about foreclosure, divorce, cancer, and addiction. The world will tell us second marriages fail 70 percent of the time as we consider getting re-married or that credit never recovers after a foreclosure. What's your battle?

At some point in your battle, when you conclude you're outgunned and outmanned, remember the God we serve is bigger than any problem we face. In one of the shortest verses in the Bible, Paul says we should

Pray without ceasing—1 Thessalonians 5:17 KJV

Don't listen to the negative artillery flashing all around the battlefield. Most of it is too far away to be anything other than a flash and a boom. And just keep firing until the enemy stops coming.

9

RESILIENCY IS EVERYTHING

n the course of writing a book or a blog, I often shift over to social media to read posts and generally break up this "PT course for the brain" known as writing. Recently, I saw a post from a good friend and ministry buddy asking for prayer. My friend's wife was just diagnosed with breast cancer and I completely blew it. Instead of praying, my thoughts raced off to *What if it was my wife?* and quickly escalated to *What would I do if I lost her?* Before too long, I was a wreck and I still hadn't prayed a word to cover my friend.

Not to sound cavalier but life happens. And sometimes it shakes the very foundation of our lives, whether it's a bad doctor's report or that all-too-common meeting in the boss's office where we learn our services are no longer needed. Before we even get out of the chair or hang up the phone, we're in a tailspin. The barrage of "What Ifs" and "Now What's" overrun our perimeter and we're suddenly fully engaged in the battle of the mind.

The enemy, by the way, loves it when our circumstances take us out of commission—the longer, the better. The longer we stay focused on the problem at hand, the less likely we are to access the full power of who we are in Christ. And pragmatically, the more consumed we are by the issue, the more time we are disengaged from everything else requiring our attention.

It's called "harassing fire" in combat, designed to make a bunch of noise, fire a lot of rounds in our direction, and has little to no aim. It just comes at us so fast we take our eyes off everything else and the mission, and our forward movement stalls.

Simply put, it's okay to get rattled by life. The trick is to not let it keep you down for long. Don't let today's situation paralyze tomorrow's potential. As countercultural as it sounds, it's okay to call a "time out" to regroup but getting back in the game is non-negotiable. Paul wrote something on this point to the Romans:

Be joyful in hope, patient in trouble and persistent in prayer

Romans 12:12

Shortly before 11 a.m. on Sunday, November 14, 1965, the first elements of the 1st Battalion of the 7th U.S. Cavalry arrived at LZ X-Ray. Aboard the first "lift," or flight, of Hueys, were men from Bravo Company, commanded by Captain John Herren, accompanied by LTC Moore and his command team. When the helicopters flared into the LZ, much of Bravo Company remained centered in the landing area, while several elements of the company were sent to the perimeter to recon the area.

Under the command of Lt. Henry "Hank" Herrick, 2nd Platoon, Bravo Company of the 1/7 CAV, was selected to begin the reconnoiter of the area adjacent to the landing zone. According to his commander, Herrick was sometimes known of his "ready, fire, aim" mindset, which was both a strength and a weakness. He was a hard-charger and a strong leader, but occasionally moved too quickly to evaluate consequences or anticipate reactions of both his team and the enemy combatants. After becoming separated from the other elements of the battalion already on the ground, Herrick opted to lead his platoon across a clearing in pursuit of a North Vietnamese squad who'd been firing on Bravo Company. An intense firefight erupted and the twenty-nine members of B Company, 2nd Platoon found themselves first flanked and then ultimately completely surrounded by enemy soldiers.

Forming a small defensive perimeter around a knoll in the clearing, the pinned down platoon, who are sometimes incorrectly called the "Lost Platoon," weren't even able to dig foxholes as some of their entrenching tools (shovels) had the handles blown off by enemy fire. I should mention here, according to any of the men from that platoon, they were the "Cut Off Platoon." In fact, if you call them the "Lost Platoon," they'll stare you down and say, "We were cut off. We were never 'lost.' We knew exactly where we were and our guys knew where we were. They just couldn't get to us." Regardless what you call them, within the first twenty-five minutes of contact, five men were killed, including Platoon Leader Herrick.

Ultimately, a young sergeant from Alabama named Ernie Savage assumed command of the platoon, after Herrick and two senior platoon sergeants were killed. Although the platoon Sergeant First Class was still alive, Savage took the lead due to his proximity to the radio. By the time Savage began calling in artillery fire on their position, eight men in 2nd Platoon Bravo were dead and an additional fifteen were wounded.

Over two days, two separate attempts were made by Company Commander John Herren to rescue what was left of his platoon. The first attempt ultimately ended in a stalemate, resulting in elements of both Alpha and Bravo Companies withdrawing. It wasn't until after the battalion used a powerful combination of artillery fire and close air support, Savage and the remnant of the "Cut Off Platoon" were ultimately recovered and relieved.

There are some powerful points in the movie *We Were Soldiers*, but none quite so well illustrated as the fate of the "Cut Off Platoon" woven through the fabric of the three-day battle sequence. While training at Fort Benning, Savage was instructed by Moore to "learn the job of the man over you, and to teach your job to the man below you in rank," and Savage executed it flawlessly.

After his rescue, Savage, along with Private Galen Bungum were regrouping at the Headquarters area on the battlefield. Upon learning the enemy was preparing to make one last, all out effort to take down the 1st Battalion, 7th Cavalry, Savage and Bungum walked over to Moore and said, "request permission to rejoin the line."

Ernie Savage retired from the Army as a Sergeant First Class in 1982, after a twenty-year career. He assumed command of a platoon after his superiors died and he kept his team alive for two days with broken shovels, no foxholes and even canteens emptied of water after stopping enemy bullets. He didn't question his job, nor did he give up.

After two days in the dirt and the loss of nine men (and an additional thirteen wounded) from Bravo Company, all SGT Savage wanted to do was get back in the fight. That's what I mean by being resilient. We have to bounce back from the attack and get back in the fight, no matter how tired we are. Regardless how bad things are, people are counting on you.

During many of my interviews, I asked members of Moore's Battalion and his family what some of the General's most popular sayings were. Our parents all have those statements they make, which we ultimately end up saying ourselves decades later. One of Hal Moore's favorites?

*Three strikes and you're not out. There's always one more thing
you can do to influence any situation in your favor.*

My wife loves to use this line on me, by the way. In the span
of my "career" as a father, I've run up against innumerable roadblocks with my kids. Anyone who's had teenagers knows they
usually do the exact opposite of what we parents suggest and
mine were certainly no exception.

In fact, at one point, my frustration with trying to engage
them in a relationship ended in me lamenting, "They don't want
me in their lives." But my wife would hear nothing of it, saying,
"You can't just give up. Just keep trying to raise them up and
teach them life lessons. You're their father."

Just recently, I was finally able to clarify my feelings to her,
by simply saying "I didn't quit. They fired me." Her response?
"You know what Hal Moore says. 'There's always one more
thing you can do. Just keep trying.'"

Now, I'm not a big fan of getting relationally punched in
the face over and over again. But my wife is tenacious. She'll
keep pounding away in the hopes of finally making some head-
way but my threshold for rejection is much shallower than hers.
"If they don't want to hear my advice, then why would I keep
talking about the same thing?" I usually reply.

It dawned on me Moore's statement is not one of resolve
when circumstances never change. He doesn't mean you keep
beating your head against the same wall in the hopes you'll
eventually punch a hole through it. That would be the definition of insanity if you think about it. In fact, it wasn't until I
spoke to Moore's son, Steve, at length about the statement
I finally understood what his father meant by it.

"Battle evolves," Steve informed me. In other words, as elements shift during the fight, doors open that weren't even there
minutes before. Do you remember Barry Sanders, the running

back from the Detroit Lions? That guy would make ten lateral cuts before he even crossed the line of scrimmage. Often, it looked like the guy was about to run headlong into a half dozen very large defensive lineman and linebackers when, quite suddenly, a tiny hole would open up and he would dart through it for a twenty-yard gain. As the play evolved, where there once stood an immovable wall of defenders, a hole opened.

Just like battle or a game like football, God has to move the right people into the correct positions for that hole to open. It may look like "strike three" but if you wait a little longer, a seemingly insignificant change will result in an opening that wasn't there the day, or even the minute before. In my own life, knowing I am clearly the "wrong man for the job" when it comes to helping some of my children make solid life choices, I repeatedly pray God brings the right person into their lives to reiterate the same things I've been saying all along. And then they'll finally understand.

If the job just isn't working out like you'd planned, just wait as God works behind the scenes. Maybe a better job will come "out of nowhere," or the source of your discontent will be moved to another department. I've seen men who stand on the fringes of life, uninvolved with almost everything that matters suddenly get rattled into action by a cancer scare. As their wives pray relentlessly for their husbands to get in the game, a simple shift in priorities comes from the terrifying fear of loss, and they're back in the battle. Often, one little adjustment by God can effect exponential change. In fact, He often works that way.

Through it all, when life kicks us in the teeth, we get back up. We fall seven times and get back up eight.

For though the righteous fall seven times, they rise again

Proverbs 24:16a

After being rescued, Sergeant Savage brushed the dirt off of his BDU's and asked permission to re-enter the fight with no regard for his own safety. And like his teammates, he'll tell you he's no hero; he just did his job. I think James says it best:

Blessed is the man who remains steadfast under trial

James 1:12

So let me ask you a question. Are you facing a seemingly hopeless situation? What's a reasonable amount of time to stay down? Have you given up because nothing's changing? What's the expiration date on feeling sorry for yourself about what happened (I know that question sounds ridiculous; we can't stay down forever, so we must have some idea of how long we're going to stay disengaged, right?).

More importantly, are you ready to get back in the fight now?

10

ESTABLISH SUPPRESSIVE FIRE SUPPORT

Years ago, I made a nearly 2000 mile trek across the country to apologize to my father for two decades of me just being an idiot. There's really no kind way to put it because that's what I was. An idiot. Rather by accident, I learned I was responsible for our relational meltdown, and decided to fly to the West Coast to say "I'm sorry."

However, between me and that apology spanned about six weeks of waiting and a speaking tour. Every weekend prior to the trip, I was in front of a group of men, recounting the story of how God convicted me about my father, and how I was traveling in mere weeks to say seek his forgiveness.

Needless to say, these guys were all over the country and were literally caught right in the middle of this fluid story between a man and his dad (You can read the whole story in my first book, *Rough Cut Men: A Man's Battle Guide to Building Real Relationships With Each Other, and With Jesus.*)

On the travel day to see my dad, while driving to the airport, I was barraged by hundreds of text messages and social media hits. "Praying for you and your father," read the first one, followed by "God's got this," "Good luck with your dad," etc. I lost count at about 250 different communications assuring me all of these men, from every corner of the U.S. and around the world, were praying for me. They were watching my back and were laying down prayer cover long before I even stepped aboard that plane. I had the confidence, no matter the outcome of my impromptu meeting with my dad, that a lot of good men had my back.

Well in advance of those Hueys, packed with cavalry troopers, touched down at Landing Zone X-Ray, preparations for the confrontation were being made. Five miles away from the battlefield was another small piece of ground called "Firebase Falcon" and its role in the Battle of Ia Drang was critical.

For three days, FB Falcon was the home of a battery of .105mm Howitzers, which would rain shells around the perimeter of LZ X-Ray throughout the battle. During the operation, radios from the field would call in coordinates to the Fire Support Officer on the ground at Falcon, who would deliver artillery to precise locations.

In fact, even during the initial troop landings, artillery teams timed their incoming fire around the arrival and departure of helicopters. They offered the Huey pilots less than a minute for their helicopters to insert troops and leave the LZ before resuming fire.

Through it all, the men on the battlefield were never without an impenetrable perimeter wall of fire created by those Howitzers. Amazingly, by the time the first seventy-two hours of the fight was over, more than twenty-three-thousand expended artillery shells lay on the ground at Firebase Falcon.

You know, the truth is a lot of us guys need that same kind of fire support. God never intended us to walk through this stuff alone. I had an incredible sense of peace while speaking to my father after years of fracture, not because I had some well-prepared speech (which I did, by the way) but simply because I knew I had a wall of prayer surrounding my relational battlefield before I even showed up at my parent's door.

I think it's pretty safe to say the Battle of Ia Drang would have experienced a very different outcome were it not for the incoming artillery fire from FB Falcon. But even after a constant barrage of exploding .105 shells, the men of the 1/7 CAV still found themselves in the dangerous position of being overrun by the enemy on the field. Although they had overwhelming fire support, they still found themselves in a losing scenario as the battle unfolded. That's when close air support became the game changer.

"Broken arrow," shouted the Forward Air Controller, U.S. Air Force Lt. Charlie Hastings into his field radio, "I say again, broken arrow!" That was the call made by LTC Moore when he realized his troopers on the ground were vastly outnumbered and practically surrounded.

There was no way they'd make it through this surge of enemy combatants without a whole lot of close air support. That "broken arrow" distress signal made by Hastings signaled every available aircraft to zero in on the embattled and wounded cavalry battalion. In the movie *We Were Soldiers*, Hastings informs Moore he has planes "stacked every 1000 feet, from 5,000 to 35,000 feet."

To the rescue came F-100 Super Sabre fighters and Skyraider propeller aircraft, armed with bombs, Gatling guns, and Napalm. Within a few short minutes, the tide of the battle turned in favor of the U.S. Army, thanks to a coordinated effort of Air Force close air support, artillery fire from Army Firebase Falcon, and some relentless warriors on the ground.

It probably comes as no surprise, due to combat-centric analogies I use while speaking, Memorial Day and Veteran's Day have become two of my most requested preaching days. Traditionally, the churches who ask me to deliver the Sunday morning message over a military holiday are also serving the military, either active duty military at a nearby installation or a high number of retirees who've opted to settle in their area.

Memorial Day 2018 was to be no different, where I was scheduled to speak at a church of nearly 5,000 Sunday attendees at four services. Deep in the throes of sermon preparation, I was forced to take a break on the Wednesday prior to Memorial Day to join my wife, Joni, at a follow up doctor's appointment. Evidently, there was something worthy of further discussion after a routine procedure.

"We thought what we detected initially was pre-cancerous," the doctor explained to us, "but we've determined that it skipped the pre-cancerous stage and there is cancer." Cancer? CANCER?! My mind raced as I attempted to digest this information but for some odd reason, it just wouldn't sink in. I still had to preach Saturday night and Sunday morning and there was no way this diagnosis was going to throw us off mission. My wife was even more adamant than I was about the upcoming weekend.

Under more normal circumstance, I would use an opportunity like this one to post something on social media about a battle of this magnitude but we both remained silent. In fact, we only invited a close circle of prayer warriors and friends into our up-ended life. Even now, on the other side of cancer, most people are genuinely shocked to hear about it because of the pronounced absence of any Facebook posts. But those we did engage with the information took to their knees in prayer for us.

By the weekend and having left this latest punch in the gut essentially "undigested," I preached all four services. Ultimately, I ended up processing much of the information I received at the doctor's office from the pulpit. In essence, I invited these church attendees into the "inner circle" of our new battlefront during the message.

The physical and emotional toll of the diagnosis was one thing, the financial stress was something else entirely. We were staring down the barrel of a $5,000 deductible, which we simply didn't have. But God did. After my sermon, I stood my post in the foyer, shaking hands and offering my book for sale. "How much is the book?," one man asked. I informed him it was $15.00. "I'll take one, but I want to pay $500 for it," he said. "I'm sorry, sir. What did you say," assuming he was either joking or I'd completely misunderstood him. "I want to pay $500 for it, to help your family." I was in a state of shock. "I'll pay $500 for it, too," said the next guy in line. At the end of that Sunday morning in May, God made a significant dent in the overwhelming deductible.

Then came the truly miraculous. The small team of people we shared the diagnosis with went to work for the Kingdom. "I just mailed you $5,000, because you don't need to worry about money at a time like this," read one message. "Our church would like to help you get through this," read a letter enclosing a $2,000 check. Within two weeks, God not only covered the deductible, but also two months worth of insurance premiums and our payroll for June.

You see, as God is sovereign and always knows what's coming, my June calendar was also virtually empty. I spent months lamenting the fact I wasn't even scheduled anywhere over Father's Day weekend—my "Super Bowl" weekend, so to speak. Try as I might, all the incoming speaking engagements skipped right over June. Looking at this through my Spiritual rearview mirror, I'm convinced God intentionally left that entire month blank so that I could be at home with Joni as she recovered.

And you know what? I was able to attend every single appointment and be a "nurse" at home without any financial stress. Every day, I was blessed to be able to do my daily devotionals in her hospital room, and watch *Wheel of Fortune* with her on a tiny hospital TV every night. God knew that battle was coming in advance and covered the financial and scheduling bases. And my fireteam did their jobs when I cried "Broken Arrow."

So whether you're preparing to go into divorce court, or you're in the middle of foreclosure, having men around you at all times is critical. We need men to share our burdens and buy into our missions. We need them to pray for us and us for them. Great things happen when men of common vision rally around us as we take a relational beachhead or attack being a father or husband with no regard for our own needs. When we align ourselves with God, fighting for the same things He fights for, hurting for what hurts Him, and loving as He does, we simply cannot lose.

The tactic to win whatever battle we're facing is to share the vision God gave us with our fireteam. There's no such thing as a one man team, unless you're playing ping pong. In battle, in any era, soldiers need soldiers.

Have you ever read of the tales of a guy named Jonathan in the Bible? He was King David's best friend—the same David who knocked Goliath out with a slingshot and a rock when he was a kid. Jonathan also happened to be the son of King Saul, David's predecessor who made a series of poor calls which resulted in his ultimate demise as King of Israel. Jonathan was a warrior in every sense of the word; he'd probably be a Special Forces operator if he was around today. In 1 Samuel 14, the Philistines, one of the principal enemies of Israel (and the same army Goliath fought for years earlier) is again plaguing the army of Israel.

Jonathan, being the warfighter he was, heads directly to his father to request permission to engage the enemy. It seems the Philistines are headquartered high atop a nearby cliff, overlooking the Israelite army, and passing the hours yelling taunts at Israel. And Jonathan is, frankly, over it. Unfortunately, his father, King Saul, isn't quite as zealous about chasing down the bad guys, opting instead to just avoid any unnecessary conflict altogether.

So Jonathan decides to grab his armor bearer and head over to the Philistine outpost. Back in this era of warfare, the armor bearer was the young guy who hauled the soldier's gear and kept it all in working order—he was like a warrior's roadie, you could say. Without objection, the armor bearer loads up and follows Jonathan across a narrow pass with Philistine overwatch positions on both sides. In fact, not only does his young armor bearer follow without question, he is solidly committed to Jonathan's mission:

'Do all that you have in mind,' his armor-bearer said. 'Go ahead, I am with you heart and soul.'

1 Samuel 14:7

Well, the Philistines are dumb enough to call Jonathan and his armor-bearer up to the outpost and the two men rout the enemy. They fought as a two-man team. And won.

Any successful campaign utilizes multiple elements to achieve victory. Without a solid perimeter of artillery, coupled with aircraft standing ready to provide close air support when called, outnumbered soldiers on the ground don't stand a chance. Sure, they may hang on for a while but in order to maintain dominance in battle, it takes a multi-pronged attack. The 1st Battalion of the 7th Cavalry survived nearly seventy-two hours in the Ia Drang Valley of South Vietnam because of a lot of shells, massive air-to-ground support, and the undaunted will to win.

Before we venture into uncharted battlegrounds in life, we should prepare in a similar fashion. Frankly, I can't recall a time in my life as a Christian man where I've gone into a major funding meeting, spoken at an event or even gone into court-mandated mediation to argue about my past due credit card balance (yeah, that happened) without first letting my fireteam buddies know what's going on.

It's funny, because we will even text each other something like "I really need the .105 today," meaning "It's time to fire in the advanced prayer artillery because I'm going to war." With that simple call, two things happen. First, a bunch of guys hit their knees, standing in the gap for me, crying out to God simultaneously. Honestly, how can God ignore that much noise? And second, I end up covered in the "peace of God that surpasses all understanding." Even if I lose, I win.

Then there are those times in my life, like when my wife was diagnosed with cancer, when even the advanced prayer artillery doesn't quite cut it, and I end up overwhelmed in the middle of a battle. But, as with the proactive prayer, I can pick up the phone and scream "Broken Arrow," and I know my brothers will answer the call and keep me covered.

Are you under fire right now? Before you rocketed forward into whatever the circumstance is, did you call for prayer support in advance? Or is the battle so bad you just need a good prayer strafing from your brothers to lessen the mounting damage? It's never too late to call them, you know.

And make sure you're checking the situation with the other guys on your team. If a buddy asks for prayer, commit to it, and do it. You may just be the only man laying down cover for him.

CHAPTER

11

MAINTAINING YOUR HEADQUARTERS

As coincidental as it may seem, I'm also good friends with a recent former commander of the 1st Squadron of the 7th U.S. Cavalry—since they're now a recon unit, they are no longer called a battalion, but it's the same battalion that fought in the Ia Drang. Along with a different role in theater, there have been changes in other parts of the Squadron as well, with "Companies" becoming "Troops." This new iteration of the 600 plus soldier unit, now based at Fort Hood, Texas, even uses a different alphabetical designation for the Troops. Alpha is now "Apache", Bravo is "Blackhawk," Charlie is "Comanche," and Delta is "Darkhorse." But no Squadron is combat ready without "Hellfighter," which is the HHT or "Headquarters and Headquarters Troop." In the Battle of Ia Drang in 1965, they were simply known as the "HHC" or Headquarters Company.

On the battlefield and even on post when the unit isn't deployed, the Headquarters Company houses some critical elements. Command can be found there, as well as primary communications, medical and supply elements, all flying under the unit guidon. Much like artillery and close air support, the HQ is a vital component in any successful operation.

And, just like the leader discussed back in the "We Are The Target" chapter, if the HQ goes down, the battle becomes a lot more challenging, if not impossible. The field command, radios, signals, maps, plans, ammo, and even medical supplies are all gone if headquarters goes down. Did you ever play Capture the Flag as a kid? Defeating the OPFOR and taking their guidon from their headquarters was the goal of the game, just as it is in warfare.

When I was first given the idea for this book, my initial mission was to point toward LTG Hal Moore as the principal character responsible for the success of the Battle of Ia Drang. But the more time I spent with the other Garryowen guys, it became evident every soldier, regardless of rank, was a key player on the field. This was clarified while interviewing a man named Carmen Miceli, a rifleman from Alpha Company, 1/7. Just like Will Parish, Miceli completed a tour in Vietnam and left the Army in 1966, ultimately spending over two decades as a fire-fighter in New Jersey.

During a very casual interview over dinner at the LZ X-Ray Reunion in 2013, I posed the question I'd come there to ask every trooper from that battle: "What was Hal Moore like?" It had yet to sink into my laser-focused mind that every one of these guys were heroes in their own right, so my line of questioning invariably defaulted directly to Moore.

When I asked Carmen to tell me about his commander, he looked at me sideways. "David," he said, staring at me like I had three heads, "I was an enlisted guy and he was our battalion commander. I saw him when he addressed the battalion at meetings, and that's about it." And then to emphasize how clearly confused I was, he added, "I wasn't even near him during the battle. My position was on the other side of the landing zone. All I was concerned about was my twelve by twelve square area."

Clarifying his point, Miceli reiterated that his only mission was protecting the six feet between himself and the guy to his left and the six feet over to the man to his right. His job on the battlefield was to ensure the enemy didn't find a gap in the line; each man defended his twelve linear feet of space in that line. In the book of Nehemiah, the key character is a young man who was born in exile in Babylon. After hearing the walls of Jerusalem, his hometown, were broken down, the man wept and decided he should be the one to rebuild it. Keep in mind this kid was born in a foreign country and had never even seen Jerusalem, yet he requests permission from the king to go "home" and fix the busted wall and gates. Nehemiah gets the king's blessing, grabs a couple of friends and heads out in the middle of the night to cast the vision of rebuilding the wall. His friends buy into the construction project and they ultimately set out to put everything back in place around the Holy City.

Structurally, it should be noted the original completed wall around the ancient City of David was ultimately about 2.5 miles around, had an average height of about thirty-nine feet and was roughly eight feet thick. There were over thirty watchtowers around its perimeter and eight separate gates providing access in and out of Jerusalem. Both King David and his son, Solomon, took part in building and expanding the series of original walls and it took decades to construct.

Nehemiah's task of rebuilding the wall was not without opposition, as is often the case with any God-inspired vision. First came those pesky naysayers, then the offensive comments, and finally an all-out physical attack on Nehemiah and his team. In fact, the attacks become so intense:

Those who carried materials did their work with one hand and held a weapon in the other, and each of the builders wore his sword at his side as he worked.

Nehemiah 4:17

In spite of a constant barrage of verbal and physical assaults, Nehemiah and his men completely rebuilt the wall in a short fifty-two days; that's the equivalent of baseball spring training season. So how did these men accomplish, in less than two months, what it took multiple kings decades to complete? First, it was God's vision and His plan. What He sets in motion won't fail. But if we look at the logistical, as opposed to the spiritual, you'll find in Nehemiah 3 that each man primarily focused on making repairs in front of his own home.

Like Nehemiah, Carmen Miceli only focused on his part of the battle line. By staying dialed in on his twelve linear feet of fighting front, connected to brothers on either side, the defense was solid. And just like both Nehemiah and Carmen, separated by nearly 2500 years, we must first focus on our homes. I don't care if you're a farmer or a firefighter, the people who need us the most are the ones right under our own roof.

As leaders, our home is our "headquarters tent." If you don't take care of your HQ, the rest of the battle is in jeopardy. I make a habit of telling the guys I meet in ministry, whether a pastor or just a man who attends, this simple truth:

Your ministry to others is only as good as your ministry at home.

In other words, you can spend all day working like a beast at your chosen career but if your home life isn't locked down and squared away, it's all for naught. Losing a marriage over a career is never a good trade-off.

However, there are ways to solidify your role as a leader at home, without compromising your time on the job or your effectiveness as a business leader. I think we should address some key principles of leadership at home I learned, quite coincidentally, as I interviewed the men of the 1/7 CAV.

12

MANAGING MULTIPLE FRONTS

At the outset of this book, I mentioned that much of what LTG Hal Moore did on the battlefield, he also replicated at home. After all, good leadership is good leadership, regardless of the venue. And as we drill into our own lives, we must first come to the realization that, like it or not, we are leaders. Or more aptly put, we are *called* to be leaders; it is entirely up to each of us whether we accept the call or not.

To give you a good illustration, I thought it would be enlightening to first share a series of quotes from different people impacted by the life of Moore. Some are family, while others are his troopers. If you're like me, you'll find it pretty eye-opening, as there is a definite consistency in Moore's actions, regardless of the "area of operations."

Q: **What is his favorite saying or "catch phrase"**

A: *"Never lie, never cheat, never steal. And never tolerate anyone who does"*

Interestingly, both son David Moore and Alpha Company Commander Tony Nadal mentioned this one first. Clearly, maintaining integrity in the family and in the unit are paramount. By the way, this is also the West Point Cadet Honor Code, literally etched in stone at the Academy in several different locations around the school.

Q: **How did he handle his role as a husband?**

A: *"He loved my mother more than anything in the world"*— David Moore.

"Moore always put his wife first. He really loved her"—Bravo Company Commander John Herren.

I've heard it said one of the best ways to love your kids is to love their mother. Our children need to see how much we care for their mothers for several reasons. First, it's a sign of security for them, as divorce is statistically one of a child's greatest fears (it's actually second only to violent crime committed on a family member). Second, it models for our sons and our daughters, what it means to be a loving husband. Remember, "more is caught than taught," so they're going to do what we do regardless of what we say.

When our daughters see what Godly manhood looks like in the context of a marriage, rest assured the bar for any potential suitors will be really high. Our daughters will settle for nothing less than what they see modeled at home between Dad and Mom. On top of that, from the work standpoint, when co-workers are aware of how you feel about your bride, there are benefits as well. It reflects a solid work-home balance since your co-workers soon discover where your priorities lie. And, albeit indirectly, it also puts up a solid "anti-flirt" barrier when female co-workers realize you are completely captivated by the wife God blessed you with.

Q: How did he handle rules and discipline?

A: *"We all knew the boundaries when Dad was at home."*— *David Moore.*

"We all knew the rules, because we knew Colonel Moore wanted to keep us safe"—*Charlie Company Will Parish.*

Because of his career, especially once he became a general officer, Moore was often away from home. Both David and Steve Moore mentioned their mother was unquestionably in charge when Dad was gone. But they were also acutely aware of the rules and the potential consequences for not adhering to them, especially once Dad got home.

Discipline is a safety net creating the perception of security. Sure, our kids will never say things like "I like being grounded" but you have to admit a swat on the hand when they attempt to stick a dinner knife in an electrical outlet is far better than the alternative. Even the Bible addresses discipline in a matter of fact way:

Those who spare the rod of discipline hate their children. Those who love their children care enough to discipline them.

Proverbs 13:24

Whether on a battlefield, at the office or at home, be a man of your word. If you warn your child of a consequence and they ultimately do exactly what you told them not to do, follow through on your discipline. An empty threat will be noticed and I promise it won't be the last time they push the edge of the envelope just to see what you will or won't do.

Q: How did he feel about the men in his unit?

A: *"He understood and he loved his men."*—*John Herren.*

"He was heartbroken whenever he lost a soldier."—Grand-daughter Alida Moore.

Moore took the time to know his troopers. Take the time to know your neighbors, your co-workers, and your buddies at church. Invest in everyone. God didn't put them near you without a purpose. When I was growing up in Jacksonville, Florida, I lived on a small suburban street with three dead end side streets. That was my whole neighborhood and we knew everybody. Every Halloween, old Tom David would throw a big party and feed all of us.

Forty years later, most of my neighbors still live in the same homes, although some have passed away. But their homes are now occupied by their grandkids and Tom David's grandson still throws a party on October 31st for the street. Unlike my old stomping ground, I now live on a cul-de-sac in a neighborhood plagued by foreclosures when the housing market collapsed in 2006. Many of our neighbors are now renters and as a result, it's become pretty transient. I may know the names of two or three people but that's about it. What about you? If you don't know your neighbors, go meet them!

Isn't it amazing Hal Moore left nearly identical imprints on the lives of his command staff and troopers, and his children and grandchildren? The consummate leader needn't change his approach when the audience changes. We lead by loving, not by domination. I think it's time to drill into some tactics that will ensure success as the spiritual leader we are called to be. Because we must answer the call.

13

DEVELOPING SOLID TTP (TACTICS, TECHNIQUES, AND PROCEDURES)

W inston Churchill is credited with saying, "Those who fail to plan are planning to fail." But, when I did some research on the quote, I discovered Benjamin Franklin reputably said it first (or some variation thereof). Is there anything Benjamin Franklin didn't say at some point? Franklin should get bonus points because I swear, he always gets back-up credit for any statement we can't assign to a particular guy. Whoever said it first, the sentiment is spot on. If we don't have a strategy to lead, it's doomed before it even starts. So let's make a plan, starting with some clear objectives to ensure victory at our home headquarters.

OBJECTIVE 1: SPEND TIME

You'll find it in a lot of parenting books but it bears repeating: The way your kids (and your wife) spell "love" is t-i-m-e. Make sure you're setting aside down time, to hang out with your kids and to take your wife out on dates. David Moore, Steve Moore, and even granddaughter Alida all mentioned Hal Moore's intentionality when it came to spending time with them. In fact, his sons, who are both over fifty, specifically mentioned fishing. Even though the General's time at home was limited, he would take his kids into the mountains.

Even more important than those fishing trips is related to a story David Moore recounted to me about his father. "We always had dinner together whenever he was home," David started out, "I remember one time, Dad was at [Fort] Bragg and had to go do inspections at another barracks. The Huey he was on had a complete power failure and crashed from about 100 feet off the ground, right after takeoff. He went to the hospital and was pretty busted up but I didn't realize it. He still ended up at the dinner table, hours after crash landing." That's a die-hard dad right there. Even a helicopter crash couldn't keep him from being at the dinner table on time.

Sure, it's a lot easier to be "hit and run" at dinner time when there's work to do, soccer practice, and the usual laundry list of other commitments but have dinner together. This is where you can debrief about your day, cheer each other on and show your children what a Godly model looks like.

OBJECTIVE 2: BE CONSISTENT WITH BOTH LOVE AND DISCIPLINE.

"I'm going to count to three and you'd better get out of that cart," the man in the grocery store cautioned his young son. Then the counting commenced, "One—I'm counting—two—I'm almost to three—I mean it—you're going to get in trouble. . . ." I never heard a "three." The guy just went back to pushing the cart, while pushing discipline aside.

I'm pretty sure I've seen this a few dozen times in my life. It's usually followed by the fleeting thoughts of what would have happened had I pulled that same act with my dad. There would have been a "three" and it would have been ugly—and probably pretty painful. I always knew my Dad meant it, because like every little kid, I pushed the boundaries once. Once.

The solid battlefield leader should also strive to be a solid leader at home. Every trooper in the 1st of the 7th knew Battalion Commander Moore meant what he said. Not because he wanted to wield his command presence or power but because he cared about his men. There were rules, and there were boundaries. What's more, there were consequences when those boundaries were crossed. Period.

"There was always a standard and we always knew if we didn't live up to it," son Steve Moore told me, "That standard never changed." It wasn't often Hal Moore got mad I'm told but when he did, you knew you'd messed up. His soldiers knew nothing would make the commander more upset than when one of his soldiers died, especially if it was the result of someone's poor decision making. Moore cried when any of his men died and often mentioned how grossly unfair it was his men died and he didn't. That's a loving leader.

Similarly, Moore's five children also knew where the line was drawn. "There was no talking back to Mom," son Dave Moore said, echoing his siblings, "We knew the boundaries and we stayed within them. Dad set the standard, the structure, and all of the things that good leaders do."

Respect and discipline begin at home and begin with us. Don't ever get to "three" without a solid follow up plan. Kids learn what an empty threat is early in life and they'll carry those same expectations into the real world. Imagine not pulling over for those flashing red and blue lights in the review mirror or ignoring the rules when taking an SAT by looking at your neighbor's test sheet. Without respect for consequences and rules, I've seen in my own life just how far off the rails undisciplined young adults can venture.

Love them like there's no tomorrow, including loving discipline. It may hurt a bit, but the long-range benefits far outweigh the temporary discomfort:

No discipline seems pleasant at the time, but painful. Later on, however, it produces a harvest of righteousness and peace for those who have been trained by it.

Hebrews 12:11

OBJECTIVE 3: PAY CLOSE ATTENTION TO THE BALANCE OF WORK AND HOME

It's okay to have short runs of a ton of work. If you're an accountant, there's a pretty good chance you're working a "million" hours between January 1st and April 15th. If you're a physician or one of those guys married to a beeper when you're on call, there's a high probability you work some crazy hours, too. Not to mention those last minute, fly-out-the-door moments. But there's a time and a place for everything. God is a God of order and we should be as well.

If you've seen the movie *We Were Soldiers* (if you haven't by now, what are you waiting for?), you're no doubt familiar with CSM Basil Plumley, adeptly portrayed by Sam Elliott. Plumley was the epitome of a high-ranking combat NCO, having earned three Combat Infantryman Badges, or CIB, during his career. In case you don't know, the CIB originated just after 6 December 1941, and is earned for active ground combat as infantry, Rangers or Special Forces. Only one CIB can be earned per major war, not just a battle. In other words, if you were a soldier in Vietnam and you were shot at by the enemy on a Monday, congratulations, you just earned a CIB. If you woke up and get shot at on the next day also, you don't get another one—it's one per war.

Since its inception, the CIB has been awarded to warfighters from World War II, Korea, El Salvador, Grenada, Panama, the Gulf War, Somalia, Iraq, and Afghanistan. CSM Plumley was a paratrooper and a cavalry trooper, earning a CIB for action during World War II, Korea, and Vietnam. Only 324 men in the history of the U.S. Army have earned three Combat Infantryman Badges. Let's just say Plumley was a beast!

At home, Basil had a markedly different role. He was a husband to his wife, Deurice, for sixty-three years. He was a father to his daughter, Debbie, and a grandfather to Debbie's little girl, Carrie. While interviewing Debbie, it became clear this man's at-home legacy was not one of a war hero but one of a loving man. In fact, since most soldiers don't talk about their downrange work when they're home, his family didn't really know who Sergeant Major Plumley was (or what he did in combat) until the movie came out in 2002. Sure, they knew he was a soldier; but to them, he was just Daddy and Granddaddy.

Don't bring work home. I know that was a pretty direct statement, but it's absolutely imperative we set limits on what we bring through the door after work. Our kids don't need to feel the full brunt of a bad day at work. They've just been waiting for us to come home. They just want Daddy.

My son and I are no strangers to long periods of relational strain. We've both messed up on countless occasions in dealing with one another and I'll admit a lot of those occasions were my fault. Being on the backside of a painful season of my son going "full prodigal" on me, we've often reflected on where we each went wrong. Sometimes I drove the train off of the rails and sometimes he was the engineer. I stood by and watched as he made some horrible mistakes, knowing some of those decisions were not going to end well.

I'm sure I'm not the only father who's witnessed the impact of bad choices our children make. Honestly, there were times when I just wanted to shake some sense into the kid, and much of my counsel fell on deaf ears. When I look at my son, now in his mid-twenties and a father, I see my little boy but I also see a series of less-than-stellar choices. But when I see my little granddaughter look at him when he walks into a room, he's a hero. He's superman. There's nothing he can do wrong in the eyes of this six-year-old. That's how our children see us when we walk in the door after a day at work where everything went haywire.

A few years ago, I spoke to a group of men in North Carolina and the subject of this chapter had a clear and decisive impact on some of the attendees. I rarely get to see the "afterglow" of an event, as I'm usually on a plane within hours. But this time, I was blessed to be able to watch a streaming service from their church.

It started simply enough, with a bunch of men on couches, sharing stories from our weekend together with their families in the congregation. But the Holy Spirit did something amazing. When the microphone was passed to one gentleman, he broke down, addressed his wife and kids in the audience and apologized for taking issues from work out on them. Then, as the mic moved across the couches, man after man tearfully apologized to their kids. It culminated with the pastor following suit.

At home, you aren't "Mr. Worker" or "Dr. Help Me." You're Daddy. You're a husband. You're a disciple of Jesus and a son of the King. Jesus said it best:

Your love for one another will prove to the world that you are my disciples.

John 13:35 NLT

OBJECTIVE 4: PROTECT YOUR MARRIAGE

Let me throw a couple of verses at you. The first is from Genesis, right out of the gate when God created Eve for Adam. *That is why a man leaves his father and mother and is united to his wife, and they become one flesh.*

Genesis 2:24

Now, let's add a little New Testament with the words of the Apostle Paul:

In this same way, husbands ought to love their wives as their own bodies. He who loves his wife loves himself. After all, no one ever hated their own body, but they feed and care for their body, just as Christ does the church

Ephesians 5:28–29

Almost a decade ago, I received a call from a church acquaintance, asking to meet to discuss a ministry idea he was strongly considering. Before the waitress took our drink order, the man said, "I feel like I'm being called into ministry but God wants me to divorce my wife first." I'm sorry if you just spit your coffee out all over this page but you probably responded just like I did. And yes, I called him on it right there.

Needless to say, it was a short meeting, as most of us don't want to hear from someone who doesn't buy into our mission, even if it is way off the mark. The Bible says there is wisdom in a multitude of counselors and some guys will just keep looking until they find someone who agrees with them. It's sort of like tossing out the high and low score in figure skating, I suppose.

I'm sure you'll agree the God we know would never advocate that sort of rash, and frankly stupid, action. I know, it's a pretty radical example of the point I'm trying to make but this sort of thing happens all day long, sailing harmlessly under our radar in a much more covert fashion.

Maybe you know "the guy." Hopefully, you aren't "the guy." You're having lunch with your buddy and every time a girl walks by, you can see his eyes lock on target. Jesus says, ***But I tell you that anyone who looks at a woman lustfully has already committed adultery with her in his heart.*** **(Matthew 5:28).**

When Job was in the middle of a series of major catastrophes in his life, he inventoried his own character and noted, ***I made a covenant with my eyes not to look lustfully at a young woman.*** **(Job 31:1).** It doesn't matter if she walks by or you're staring at her on your laptop, you're in dangerous territory. Porn or in person, you might as well hit yourself in the head with a block of wood because when you said "I do" to your wife, the "two became one." You hurt you, you hurt her. And it's our responsibility to guard her heart and our own hearts at the same time.

Frankly, it doesn't even have to be a major sexual sin violation to undermine what God has put together with the two of you. I've lost count of the times I've heard men complaining about their wives in a public setting. And vice versa. Don't talk negatively to others about your spouse, ever. And never post it on social media for the whole world to see. Handle it at the HQ, but not in public.

It may not seem like a big deal but it can open the door to much greater threats to our marriages. The world is already out to take down our marriages. The last thing we need to do is elevate the threat level by being selfish, sarcastic or downright mean. Leaders don't roll that way. We are the stewards of our marriages and we must protect them at all costs.

OBJECTIVE 5: BE A UNIFIED PARENTAL FRONT

"Mom lets me play M-rated video games at her house," my then-eleven-year-old son said as he walked into the house for a weekend visit. Suddenly, I was the bad guy for having a clearly defined set of age-appropriate parameters. Over time, as he grew older, he didn't even come over anymore, simply because the rules were more flexible at the other house. This is a battle many divorced and sometimes remarried men face all the time. Regardless of whether it's an R-rated movie, a sleepover or just a poor selection of who to make friends with, there are often ideological battles between separated parents.

In truth, this type of interaction isn't just limited to divorced couples either. Kids figure out pretty quickly they can manipulate a situation by pitting one parent against the other. "Mom said it was up to you," was one I used to say all the time. "Well," Dad would say, "if it's okay with her, then it's okay with me." And I'd get my way since no one actually made a decision. Or when one made a less-than-favorable decision, I'd simply try and negotiate my way into the response I was seeking from the much easier target.

At the HQ, we need to be a unified force, period. The mission of our eighteen-plus-year time with kids living in our "headquarters tent" is to raise wise, God-fearing, adult men and women. And sometimes, as parents, we have to make unpopular decisions based upon the long-term mission, as opposed to winning favor or looking like "Superdad." Being a dad was never and will never be, a popularity contest. We can't be our kid's best friend and also be a father.

Compromising the mission in an effort to gain friend status with our kids is like parental hara-kiri. Worse yet, when one parent is trying to be a "bestie" to the children, while the other is attempting to fulfill the aforementioned mission, chaos ensues. It's no different than if Bravo Commander Herren and Alpha Commander Nadal opted to work from completely different battle plans, all the while disregarding orders from Battalion Commander Moore. Without approaching the fight as a unit, the odds of winning at Ia Drang would have been far worse.

So regardless the backlash, whining, yelling, kicking or screaming, parents must stay on the same team. Take it from a guy who failed at this very thing while attempting to co-parent in two different households. It won't end well. Remember, *If a house is divided against itself, that house cannot stand.* —Mark 3:25

OBJECTIVE 6: HOME IS A SAFE PLACE

We have an adult son with special needs, Michael, living at home with us. He has a lot of issues, both physical and mental, resulting from a day-long seizure episode when he was only a few days old. He attended a special school and may quite possibly live at home for the better part of his life. Over the decades, the cultural nickname for his disability has changed and you might even remember other kids using not-so-politically-correct terms for folks like Mike when you were in school. The more I travel, the more I meet men who have similar circumstances at home. We aren't alone.

We also have four other kids, all now in their twenties, and the oldest ones are girls. Middle school was a terrible time in all our lives, simply because kids can be so mean to each other. The "level of awful" was an "11 on a scale of 10" when the girls were in middle school.

Let me just paraphrase it like this: People can be mean. Whether it's a special needs child, a middle school student or nasty people at our offices, everyone needs a safe place to feel loved and normal.

As men, there's the constant, culturally-imposed need to look like we're on our "A-game" all the time. We have to appear as if we've got it all together at church, at work, and at meetings. This is what my wife so aptly calls "being on stage." Every actor needs to be able to pull the plug, take off the makeup and wardrobe, and just go backstage. When actors are backstage, they can be real. They can be themselves and not a character in some production. Our home headquarters should be "backstage." The minute it becomes another stage or performance venue, we're in trouble. The amazing thing about Michael is he really doesn't acknowledge that he's much different from anybody. Sure, he gets a little frustrated when his brother can tackle a higher level on a video game Mike may struggle with and he is totally cool with not being able to drive.

I've met countless men who feel compelled to keep their family on a perpetual stage and the collateral damage can be brutal. Coats and ties or makeup and heels are not necessary at the dinner table, unless you happen to be entertaining the Queen of England. Use your home HQ as a place to debrief about the day. That doesn't mean bring it all home and dump it on your family but rather just let the kids update you about their day. Ask your wife how her day went, then shut up and let her talk. She doesn't need us to fix it unless she asks; she just wants to be heard.

Our kids don't need another place forcing them to be something they're not. And frankly, neither do we. Keep your home a safe place to be real and for everyone to feel loved for exactly who they are. There's no acting when you're backstage. Just be you and let them be them.

OBJECTIVE 7: GUARD YOUR LEGACY

Let's face it; we're all leaving a legacy. It's officially up to us what that legacy will be. No matter how you look at the trail we're leaving behind, kids will eventually walk in our footsteps. For some of us, we've even radically changed directions later in life and we need to ensure our children shift directions along with us. Being a later-in-life convert myself, my kids had first-hand experiences with both the unsaved "Dave" and the new and improved, Christ-centered "David." When my mission shifted, I had to make certain I passed the orders down the line so the Godly legacy I was attempting to build from the ashes of my pre-salvation life would be carried on to the next generation.

During my interviews with the LZ X-Ray family, I had the pleasure of engaging with Alida, Hal Moore's granddaughter. She's the daughter of the General's daughter Julie, lives in Seattle, and was recently married, but at the time we spoke, her last name was Moore. Without going into great detail about her life, Alida's biological father left the family when she was only three months old. As a result, Alida and Julie moved in with Hal and Julia Moore (aka- Mom and Dad) for a period of time.

It was during this time the General and Joe Galloway were working on the book *We Were Soldiers Once, and Young*. Alida says, since it took ten years to write the book and the men started writing prior to her birth, both the book and her "Granddaddy" were always a part of her life.

For that period of time in Alida's life, Hal Moore played the dual role of father and grandfather. In fact, much of what she will tell you about her grandfather is a mirror image of what Moore's children say. She says her grandfather had "boundless energy," recalling fond memories of spending time together, laughing, fishing, and even playing with the family Dalmatian (the General actually wrote a poem about that dog). And while most of us refer to Moore by the call sign "Garryowen 6" (the "6" in the call sign is usually the commander of the unit), to Alida, his call sign was just "Captain Fun."

Something struck me as Alida and I were talking; it was really more logistical in nature than anything but I had to ask. "Why is your last name Moore?" I inquired. You may think it's a goofy question but stay with me for a minute. Alida is a daughter of Hal Moore's daughter and traditionally, when a woman gets married, she takes the last name of her husband. Alida's mother did take her husband's name prior to his early departure from the marriage, and even if she had reverted to her maiden name, Alida's name should have been that of her biological father. But it wasn't.

"When I got older," Alida told me, "I decided that I wanted to know more about my father, so I tracked him down." Now, I am not at liberty to speculate on what happened, nor did Alida elaborate on what exactly went down but she made a decision after that meeting. She opted to go to the courthouse and legally change her last name to Moore. When I asked her why, her reply was crystal clear, "Because I wanted my name to mean something."

The Bible talks of legacy, and names, in Proverbs 22:1:

A good name is more desirable than great riches; to be esteemed is better than silver or gold.

Are we living a life worth repeating? What does it mean to have our last name? Every day, we should keep our focus on making sure who we say we are lines up with who we say we are in Christ. We should all want our name to "mean something." Guard your legacy.

OBJECTIVE 8: COVER YOUR WIFE IN PRAYER EVERY DAY

I'm not entirely sure I need to elaborate too much on this one but praying for your wife should be an integral part of team synergy. It's like laying down covering fire for her every day. Sure, she may have a great ladies' group praying for her but you're her husband. There's something exponentially more impactful about a husband praying for his wife. Yes, it's great to pray *with* her, but I'm talking about high impact, prayer closet caliber praying for that woman! I'll just leave it at that.

Admittedly, that was a lot of ground to cover in a single chapter. And if you're like me, you've already been convicted by one or more of those daunting objectives. Even as I'm writing, I'm getting punched in the gut by a few things I could do differently. But before you get all overwhelmed, let me narrow a path to success into three overarching bullets that will make it a whole lot more attainable.

- First, don't try to address everything at once. The mission is to be just 1 percent better than yesterday. Frankly, making a dozen radical changes at once could cause everyone in the house to scratch their collective heads. They won't know how to take it and if they're like most people, they'll be counting the minutes until we're right back to the same old guy. Just like a fitness regimen, it's all about repetition and discipline. You won't drop twenty pounds on a single bike ride; you lose weight when you stay at it

- Second, your chances of making solid changes increases by a factor of a few hundred if you have a battle buddy committed to support you, encourage you, and even hold you accountable. Share the mission before you start, then set periodic checkpoints throughout the journey. Be honest with the guy. If you've committed to begin praying for your wife, don't get all bent out of shape if he asks if you prayed for her today. That's his job. Your success is his mission and vice versa

- Third, and most important of all, none of this will fly if God isn't involved. Without Him, it's just behavior modification. Pray that He reveals the biggest choke points and allow Him to begin working on a heart change. It takes a lot of years to create bad habits and they're all-but-impossible to break without God. We can do some of it by sheer force of will, but it won't be sustainable over the long haul.

Pray, get a wingman, and take it a day at a time. And if the whole concept of God's involvement is throwing you a little, read on.

CHAPTER

STAY CONNECTED TO THE COMMAND CHOPPER

While it may appear the troopers of the 1st Battalion of the 7th U.S. Cavalry were all alone on the battlefield, there were support elements all over the place. You're already aware that a mere five miles away was Firebase Falcon, pounding the perimeter with artillery. In nearby waters were aircraft carriers launching air support and helicopters armed with aerial rocket artillery came from surrounding positions. But there's another component of the battle often overlooked, especially in the movie rendition.

Days before the initial landing at LZ X-Ray and the launch of Operation Silver Bayonet, LTC Moore and a team of men flew high over the prospective landing area to do recon. Moore was joined by his boss, 3rd Brigade Commander Colonel Tim Brown. During the days of close contact with the PAVN and NVA regulars, Operations officer, Captain Gregory "Matt" Dillon circled above the battlefield in a Huey. From his perspective, he was able to see enemy troop movements, PAVN positions and even wires indicating enemy radio positions the men on the ground were unable to see due to vegetation,

Elephant grass and hills. While the troopers couldn't see ten feet ahead, Dillon had a bird's eye view of the entire theater of operations, and similar to a coach in the press box during a football game, he was able to orchestrate the battle from an elevated position.

Iconic names in football, both college and professional, are a staple in any sports related conversations among men. Johnny Unitas, Joe Namath, Peyton Manning—we all know the names and many of us know their jersey numbers, player statistics, and even the years they played. My guess is very few men have ever heard of David Daniels.

David Daniels was a standout wide receiver at Penn State University in the late 1980's and early 1990's. Playing his high school ball in Sarasota, Florida, he was recruited by the likes of the University of Florida, Florida State University, and Miami, but chose instead to play college ball under the legendary Joe Paterno.

After a stellar career in the NCAA, David was drafted in the third round by the Seattle Seahawks, where he played for two years, until his career ultimately came to a premature end due to a back injury. I have the distinct pleasure of calling this man of God my friend and we occasionally have lunch together. Since I am such an avid fan of football, but a relative novice when it comes to the inner workings of the professional game, I asked him a question which transformed the way I see how we, as men in the church, communicate with each other and with God: "How does the game change when you are inside the Red Zone?"

By definition, the "Red Zone" is the area on the field inside your opponent's twenty-yard line. In other words, you are about to score. "The field becomes eighty yards shorter. Everything becomes more intense," David said, "and faster. There is no time to react and you need to pay attention. Your thinking speeds up, the routes you run are more abrupt, and the communication between everyone gets more detailed. And the defense throws stuff at you that you don't see over the other eighty yards of the field."

The whole concept of communication also fascinates me, both on and off the field. On the field, there is a huddle between each play, where the quarterback gives each player their deployment plans for the upcoming assault on the defense. While the huddle is what we see on television, there is a barrage of instructions coming from the sideline coaches, as well as "the guy upstairs"—the offensive coordinator, sitting in the press box with a bird's eye view of the entire field. Each component is critical for every down played. The quarterback sees things from the field perspective and the coaches on the sidelines are the strategists, but absolutely every play revolves around the viewpoint of that man in the press box.

"Did you know that the coach in the press box takes pictures, and video, of every down and every formation?" David informed me. "He looks at each position individually and sees things with the defensive formation that we would never see on the field. Maybe a cornerback is standing too far back every time, which means there is a weakness there. Or a blitz comes from that particular formation every time, so be ready. Every play originates from that guy in the box."

"One thing I always knew," David said, "was that I couldn't trust my field view."

Our lives as men of God are designed to replicate what we see on the field every single weekend. If you want to score while you are in the Red Zone, a great deal of communication needs to happen. There are rules to the game of life and without constant communication from both the guys in our huddle, and God, we often set ourselves up for failure without even seeing failure coming. "Sometimes, the defense that you see on the field looks like a zone defense, but the guy upstairs tells you it's man-to-man," my friend David shared, "and if the coach on the field ignores what the guy in the press box tells him, then the defense will intercept a pass or sack the quarterback for a loss almost every time."

Unlike the Red Zone on a football field, the battlefield is, literally do or die. It's not about scoring a quick six points, but rather keeping teammates alive. Situational awareness is critical, ensuring the ability to react quickly to an ever-changing theater. And honestly, without a solid overhead view, a soldier in contact is at a huge disadvantage. Unlike football, what may be lurking on the other side of the grass doesn't want to tackle him—it wants to kill him.

Understand, I'm in no way likening an inconsequential game like football to real world combat, so don't be coming at me with that! But there is a striking similarity in the need for different perspectives of the field, especially a high-altitude view.

In order to win on the field, we must stay linked up with the command chopper. In our world, as Christian men fighting an enemy who wants us out of the battle, it's critically important to be in constant communication with God. God is our command chopper as we "do life." Obviously, radios aren't an option to speak to Him but there's always an open line through prayer. If you're anything like me, prayer can often be a challenge but it's frankly impossible to establish our bearings if we're not talking to God. He's our Commander and He can see the entire dark road when we can barely see past the high beams.

God doesn't need our prayer in fancy King James English or in some undecipherable Christian code. It's just a conversation, just like ones we'd have with our wives, kids or co-workers. Maybe it's been a while for you? Or maybe you've never even attempted to get off a "comm shot" to God in the middle of battle. You're not alone, as even Jesus's original Disciples weren't sure what to do or even how to say it:

One day Jesus was praying in a certain place. When he finished, one of his disciples said to him, 'Lord, teach us to pray.'

Luke 11:1

If you're getting beaten up right now, set this book down and make that call to the Command Chopper. You can even be mad; God can take it. But don't continue to fight at ground level with no input from the One who sees it all, created it all and most importantly, wants us to win this firefight we're in.

Call to me and I will answer you and tell you great and unsearchable things you do not know.

Jeremiah 33:3

CHAPTER

15

BROTHERHOOD

As I mentioned a few pages ago, there are three keys to success in the mission of manhood. The first was pretty self explanatory, with the goal being nothing more than slow but steady improvement in the arenas of marriage and fathering. And while staying connected to the chopper above the battlefield is the primary lifeline, the need for a solid friend is nearly as invaluable.

Nowhere is brotherhood more adeptly illustrated than on the battlefield. A lifetime bond forms between men regardless of how long that lifetime may be. When the only thing that really matters is protecting your co-combatants and the only mission is survival, something changes between two men. There's no better way to cast a bright light on my definition of friendship than to share a story of two of the men from Ia Drang.

The year 2015 marked the fiftieth anniversary of the Battle of Ia Drang (and the Vietnam War), and my wife and I spent three days celebrating with the veterans of Garryowen in Charleston, South Carolina. During a dinner at the Citadel, we had the pleasure of being seated with John Rangel and his wife, Shirley, and a wonderful family we hadn't met at previous reunions. During the course of dinner, buried in the midst of the usual "getting to know you" questions, an amazing story of lifelong brotherhood surfaced. A story I'd never heard and one definitely worth re-telling five decades later. The following excerpts are taken directly from memories written by John Rangel in 2004:

Jack Gell and I were stationed at Fort Benning, Georgia. We knew each other then, but did not get to really know each other until we shared the same cabin aboard the ship that was taking us to Vietnam. At night, we talked a lot about our families and how much they meant to us, and how hard it had been to leave them, and how much we missed them. He told me about his wife Becky, his little girl Bonnie, his son Jay and his baby girl Carol. He also told me that they had stayed in Columbus, Ga. I told him about my wife Shirley, my son Steve (2 years old) and my son David, who was 10 months old. Since Shirley and the boys were staying in Columbus too, we thought it would be a good idea for the two of them to meet. I wrote to Shirley and told her about Sgt. Gell's wife and the children. I suggested that she look her up.

When we docked in San Diego, he went ashore and met with his mom. He was very happy to see her and spend some time with her. He was one of the few who actually got to meet with family members on that stop. I have often thought about how special it was for him to be able see his mom before we continued on our way to Vietnam.

As we continued on our journey, we would talk about our mission and how we felt about what we were doing. We felt we were doing the right thing and we were both so glad that our families were safe in the United States. Neither of us knew anything about war, except that we had been training for it. We knew the situation was very serious and there was a possibility that we might not make it back home alive.

When our ship finally docked in Vietnam and we were ready to leave our cabin, we exchanged these words "If something happens and I don't make it back, will you look after my family?" We told each other that we would do this. We both cried as we shook hands and embraced each other. Then we left to join the rest of the men on deck.

On November 14th, 1965, Sergeant Jack Gell was killed in the Ia Drang Valley. I was wounded and then sent to Letterman General Hospital in San Francisco. Three months later, when I was released from the hospital and went back to Columbus, Ga. I met Becky and the children for the first time. We have a very special friendship. Shirley and Becky are best friends, our children are like brothers and sisters. They became a part of our family and we love them dearly.

I will close by saying, "Happy Birthday my friend and you will never be forgotten."

John Rangel, Jr.

Knowing they may never see their families again, Rangel and Gell made a commitment that would never be broken. To put things in proper perspective and to fill in a couple of gaps in Rangel's letter, you should know the voyage to Vietnam, aboard a Merchant Marine ship originated in Charleston, SC, took over a month to complete. And while I don't know how long the two men were training together at Benning, I do know it was the common mission that bound them together.

The upcoming war in Vietnam, probably peppered with a great deal of fear of the unknown, created a rock-solid connection between Rangel and Gell. Men get connected when they share common life experiences. When we spill the same blood in the same mud—whether in war, divorce, bankruptcy or marriage—a nearly impenetrable bond is forged.

It's been over a decade since Rangel penned those thoughts and the "rest of the story" is as equally compelling and impactful. Fifty years have passed since those two men made a covenant with each other. Jack Gell's kids are all grown up, with kids of their own, and his wife has since remarried. But, through it all, the Rangels and the Gells have been connected permanently.

At the reunion dinner, John shared with us the final piece of the mission commencing in the cabin of that ship in 1965. "A while back," he said while tearfully looking around the table at Jack Gell's family, "Shirley and I took Becky and all of the kids to the cemetery where Jack is buried. With his family behind me, I snapped to attention, saluted to my friend, and said, 'Jack, mission accomplished'. He asked me to watch over his family and I did. No questions asked."

My friend, I don't think I could fabricate a more lucid illustration of the urgent need we have in our lives for that one friend. Neither Gell nor Rangel asked the other for specifics like "How long are we talkin' here?" when it came to that level of commitment. Neither man shook it off and said "Don't worry, bro. You'll be fine." Isn't it funny how often we do that when faced with a truly monumental threat to our finances or even our lives?

The Bible spells out the type of friendship men need, using battle-hardened men as examples. Remember the tale of Jonathan and his armor-bearer? When warrior Jonathan met soon-to-be King David, here's how it went down:

After David had finished talking with Saul, he met Jonathan, the king's son. There was an immediate bond between them, for Jonathan loved David.

1 Samuel 18:1 NLT

In today's popular culture, the next "verse" might read something like, "Then David and Jonathan immediately surrendered their 'man cards.'" But it doesn't. Throughout the course of their friendship, David and Jonathan took turns saving each other from death. In fact, when Jonathan's father, King Saul, took an interest in ending David's life, Jonathan's loyalty resided with his buddy, not his dad.

Tactically, it's great to have a battery of Howitzers raining shells on your perimeter to keep you safe. It's also never a bad thing to have close air support relentlessly pounding the enemy. But on the ground, there's no substitute for having a man right next to you in a tight cover formation.

There are men around you. Guys you've known for years perhaps. Do you trust them enough to share your battles? To be vulnerable enough to ask for help? To trust another man to cover your six? If you were heading downrange, is there a man to whom you'd entrust your family?

If you're like a lot of men, you may not be able to answer that one. Please don't let another day go by without dropping your guard long enough to link up with another man. Without him, the enemy will eventually pick you off.

In the movie *We Were Soldiers*, as Huey lifts are flaring in and out of a hot landing zone under intense enemy fire, Moore is out in the middle of the LZ signaling the Hueys to land. Sergeant Major Plumley, runs over to his commander and yells "We have to find you some cover, because if you go down, we all go down."

If you go down, your family is next. Get some cover. Find that guy.

WRITE THE AAR

Any soldier will tell you the Army loves the AAR or "After Action Review." What originated as a way to debrief after a battle has become a daily occurrence, whether it's combat related, after a post-wide barbecue or after I come in to speak to soldiers. I've actually been the subject of quite a few AAR's in the past, whether as a keynote speaker at a Post-wide Prayer Breakfast in Germany or suicide prevention training with 1,000 junior NCO's from a Stryker Brigade. The level of intensity of the AAR varies, as I've seen some hand-written and others being full-blown multimedia storyboards with photos and video. Regardless of the media used, the intent of the AAR is invaluable.

The After Action Review is a line by line replay of whatever actions occurred. After the Ia Drang Battle, then-Lt. Col. Moore wrote down all that transpired over the three days while his unit was engaged with the enemy. Moore's LZ X-Ray AAR also includes information leading up to the action and a play-by-play for each company during contact.

There are innumerable lessons to be learned from an AAR—what went wrong, what went right, and how to do things differently are just a few of them. If new tactics or weapons are used, a review of their performance is included, as is the positioning of support elements. The goal is to learn from mistakes, to capitalize on successes, and to have an ever-changing logbook of useable, measureable data. After all, if you don't know what you did right or wrong and don't document tactics that work and those that don't, you're often doomed to repeat mistakes. Most importantly, the AAR allows you to look back on those same successes and failures at any time in the future. It's an archive of your unit's battle history.

Adhering to the overarching theme of living life in a "combat theater," we should be logging our own actions, successes, and failures as well. In Christian circles, it's called a journal and the method is pretty simple. You can pick up a journal at any bookstore for a few bucks. You can even use one of those black and white essay notebooks from middle school English class if you prefer to stay a little more covert about it. Here's at least one suggested way to systematically document life's ups and downs:

1. Get up early and spend some time listening to your marching orders. In other words, pray and listen. Hang out with God.
2. Get a good Bible reading plan. They make them for guys with serious time constraints like us. Check out the YouVersion app, which is totally customizable based upon topic and available, and will pepper you with reminders if you tend to get sidetracked like me.
3. Date your book and write down what you hear. What hits your heart? What is He revealing to you?
4. Write down your prayer needs. All of them, regardless of how overwhelmingly big or underwhelmingly miniscule.

5. Make sure you go back and log whenever those prayers are answered. You'd be stunned how often God does something incredible. We just have really bad spiritual amnesia sometimes.
6. Log any major roadblocks or relational messes too, including how they got messed up in the first place. And pray about them.
7. Keep your books on a shelf. When you burn through one, get another. Don't stop logging.
8. Every so often, just grab one and read through old pages. It's a great reminder of how far you've come.

Remember, if we don't write things down, how can we know if we're even on the right path? Or how far we've already come? Every business has a budget, a vision statement, and measureable data to see if they're even a viable company. Every unit, even Chaplains and cooks, fill out AAR's after every action. And every Bible believing warrior for Christ needs to journal. It's a non-negotiable element of successful battles.

Try it for a few weeks. It'll change everything!

DEPLOYMENT READINESS— THE BACK BRIEF

t's a drill no one is really a big fan of—the Deployment Readiness Exercise. When the current 1st Squadron of the 7th U.S. Cavalry goes through one, it includes rolling giant M-1 tanks and Bradley Assault Vehicles onto train cars to get them from Texas to a ship, accompanied by nearly 700 battle-ready troopers and all their gear. It all happens in a matter of hours. Just in case they are needed, the 1/7 CAV can mount up their entire unit and be deployment ready in the blink of an eye. There are layers of leadership and a ton of checklists. And double checklists.

Let's wrap this thing up by doing the same thing. It's time to deploy. No more preparation or training, gentlemen. This is a "live fire" situation and you *will* face contact. Here's your final checklist:

- Remember, we are at war with a real enemy
- Battlefield leadership translates directly to leadership at home

- The enemy wants to take you out, because if you're out, your family goes down
- The enemy will hit weaker soldiers as a distraction to take you out of the battle
- We are on enemy ground. This is not our home; it's a deployment
- We need to "armor up" every day before we move out
- It's great to be connected to an Army but it's all about the fireteam—We need a couple of men who will fight for us and with us
- We need men in our lives who will support us, encourage us, and hold us accountable when we step out of line or jeopardize the mission
- We need to know who we can count on in the battle to provide covering fire and "Close Prayer Support"
- We need to be aware of our personal "choke points"—where Satan can gain a foothold—and proactively pray against them to hit them head on
- We absolutely must let go of the past. Yesterday is over. It's a new day
- Don't pay attention to the odds and don't listen to people who say you'll fail. This battle joins you and God. Greater is He in you than he that's in the world, remember?
- Bounce back quickly. It's okay to be defeated for a day but people are counting on you to get back in the fight. The pity party is over
- Share your struggles with your battle buddy. You need suppressive fire support. A soldier fighting alone is going to go down eventually. You can't win this alone
- Maintain your household first, as it's your number one mission
- Spend time with your wife. Go on a date night. Re-engage
- Kids spell love "t-i-m-e"

- When it comes to your kids, be consistent in both your love and your discipline. Don't waver on either front
- Pay attention to how you balance work and home. Don't be a workaholic!
- Guard your marriage. Protect it. She's your wife, not your enemy
- Be a unified parental team with your wife. Kids often capitalize on, and suffer from, division
- Keep your home a safe place from the world, for your marriage and for your children. Don't bring a bad day into your HQ
- Guard your legacy. Always be aware the kids are watching. Are we modeling for them what we'd ultimately like them to become? Remember, more is caught than taught
- Pray for your wife. If you won't, who will?
- Belonging to a fireteam is great, but who's on your six? Find that one man to drag you off the field when life blows your spiritual legs off. And vice versa
- Start a journal today. It's the only way to measure results and to see just how much God is doing in your life.
- Remember, our goal is improvement. A little each day. Just shoot for being 1 percent better than yesterday.

And most importantly . . .

- Stay connected to God. He doesn't need some fancy prayer or for you to enter the priesthood. But He did create us and we are the apple of His eye. Remember, He loves us so much He sacrificed His only Son so we could gain a spot in Heaven. That's what true love is.

Sometimes, in a busy world, we lose contact with God. The mountains of life's battles have interfered with our "line of sight" communication. We get so busy we just shove Him into a corner until Sunday morning. We treat God like spiritual Alka Seltzer and only act as if we need Him when we have heartache or challenges. It's easy to do, trust me. We're double-timing it through life and suddenly we're so far ahead of or behind God we can't even see Him anymore. It's time to stop and re-establish good comms.

Maybe you've never even considered Him as an option in the midst of struggle. You've heard about Him, but perhaps you've never heard about Him in the context of battle. This is your reveille. This is your call to arms.

Whatever the case, you need to know, right now, God loves you. He is with you in this battle and wants you to win. The only thing you need to do is re-establish a line of communication. And it's all in a simple prayer you can say quietly under your breath or shout it from the rooftops. That's your call. As this book winds down, the most important thing you can do is communicate with the Lord. And here's all you really need to say:

Dear God:

I don't know how I got here, but I need You. I can't do this alone anymore. I acknowledge I'm a fallen man and need the salvation only You can give. Forgive me for my sins, Lord. Pick me up out of the dirt and make me clean again. Thank you for saving me, God. I will serve you for the rest of my life!

I pray this in the Name of Your Son, Jesus. Amen.

It's really that simple. You're done. You've successfully re-established communications with the Creator of the Universe.

You know what needs to be done. Use this book as your checklist. Go after that marriage. Be the father you've always wanted to be. Be a man of integrity and a soldier of the Most High God.

In the immortal words of Lieutenant General Harold G. Moore, Commander of the 1st Battalion of the 7th U.S. Cavalry (Airmobile), 14–17 NOVEMBER 1965. . . .

"DRIVE ON!"

21-DAY
DEVOTIONAL—
INTRODUCTION

Guys, I need to be honest about something. Sometimes I have a really hard time sticking to my spiritual disciplines. But I am really adept at making checklists, as you probably noticed in the last chapter of the book. I threw out concepts like journaling, spending time in the Word, and staying connected to God, yet I drop the ball on those way too often. My greatest challenge is when my Bible reading plan becomes another checklist.

I think, *Nice job, man. You knocked out that 4.33 chapters of the Word in record time today. You're going to be able to read through the Bible by October!*

When it comes to time with God, I know a lot of guys struggle with the same thing I do. It slowly degrades into yet another thing to do. A list to check off line by line, sort of like mowing the grass or shaving. It becomes rote and as dry as the Sahara Desert sometimes, right?

To that end, I decided to add something to the end of this book: a 21-day devotional. They say twenty-one days forms a habit, so here's a good kickstart to the spiritual disciplines. Each devotional is short, but hits on topics I've often struggled with. This way, you get to benefit from my mistakes without having to duplicate them in your own lives.

And the bonus is, if you're a checklist guy like me, you'll be happy to know you can check off "time with God" and "time in the Word" simultaneously every day!

Set aside a few minutes every day for the next few weeks and allow God to make course adjustments where needed. Grab a pen and a journal to jot down your thoughts.

I'm with you in the battle. Enjoy!

David

DAY #1

WHERE DID GOD GO?

One of my lifelong dreams has been to create a video series to align with our live "Rough Cut Men Movie Experience" content, including the Hollywood movie vignettes. I figured it would be a great way to engage a smaller group of men with the same proven material without all the expense associated with bringing in a speaker. Then my vision changed a bit, as I began speaking to more and more soldiers. At that point, the video concept morphed from a church audience to a military audience, specifically as it pertains to isolation, friendlessness, addiction, domestic violence, and even suicide. The vision was to come alongside the chaplains, giving them a turnkey eight session series for small groups, delivered via streaming content complete with downloadable facilitator's guides.

But my dream was far more elaborate than just a video series. I didn't want soldiers staring at my face behind a podium for a half hour. Sure, the clips from the movies would be embedded into each session but who wants to look at some guy behind a podium on video the rest of the time? So we set out to do something completely unique—we traveled to wherever each respective movie was filmed to capture the teaching segments.

Long story short, we filmed *Armageddon* on the floor of Mission Control at Johnson Space Center, *Forrest Gump* on the deck of a shrimp boat in Bayou La Batre, Alabama, *Rudy* in the gameday locker room at Notre Dame and we even filmed the *Saving Private Ryan* session on Omaha Beach on the north coast of France. The series turned into something beyond my wildest imagination, as we built a companion website and solicited the help of Army chaplains all the way to the Pentagon. The target release date was January 1, 2017. Or should I say, my target release date....

Two years later, the series was still waiting for its epic release. A combination of a new Commander in Chief, radical budget reconciliations and a battery of retirements (which included some of my strongest allies) left us waiting. And waiting. On more than a hundred occasions, I've suggested to our board, and my wife, that we should just release it to the church. "The Army is never going to happen," has always been my default position. And yes, as I write this devotional, the video series is still dormant yet fully operational.

When the nation of Israel was still using what we could call a "portable church," the Tabernacle was the house of worship. The Holy of Most Holy Places was located in the center, and the Tent of Meeting and surrounding curtains were both brilliantly elaborate and built to the exact specifications God gave Moses. The Levites, one of the twelve tribes of Israel, were the priests of the nation and were consequently tasked with setting up, tearing down, and transportation of the Tabernacle, along with all of its components and hardware, whenever the nation of Israel moved from one place to the next.

But the decision to move the Tabernacle was never left to speculation or guess work. Every command to move was based on one thing—the cloud of the Lord, which rested over the Tabernacle:

On the day the tabernacle, the tent of the covenant law, was set up, the cloud covered it. From evening till morning the cloud above the tabernacle looked like fire. That is how it continued to be; the cloud covered it, and at night it looked like fire. Whenever the cloud lifted from above the tent, the Israelites set out; wherever the cloud settled, the Israelites encamped. At the Lord's command the Israelites set out, and at his command they encamped. As long as the cloud stayed over the tabernacle, they remained in camp.

Numbers 9:15–18

Whenever the cloud lifted, the entire population of Israel moved. Moving wasn't exactly a simple process, as it involved hundreds of Levites packing up thousands of pounds of material comprising the massive Tabernacle. I would imagine it looked similar to setting up a present-day concert at Wembley Stadium. The tear down process would commence immediately when the cloud lifted and the arduous task of setting it all back up again would start as soon as the cloud stopped, regardless of how long the Israelites camped at a particular location.

Whether the cloud stayed over the tabernacle for two days or a month or a year, the Israelites would remain in camp and not set out; but when it lifted, they would set out.

Numbers 9:22

Just like the nation of Israel back in the days of the Tabernacle, there are really only two ways we can inadvertently end up separated from the covering and protection of the Lord. The first is when the cloud moves and we don't. The other is when we move out from under the cloud. In other words, God is either trying to do a new thing and we keep doing what we've always done; or, God hasn't moved yet, and we became impatient and move forward without Him.

Every time I suggest releasing our video series to the church, my wife reminds me of the favor God showed us with people and locations that should have been inaccessible. She also reminds me of how God provided the funding to film all over the world. "God didn't open all of those doors just to have the videos go unused," she has said more than once, "so we just need to wait."

Our tendency is to just go. Time's up and it's time to move. We've got to make something happen. Remember, it's not ours to make happen but God's. It's not our time but rather His. Look around at your life right now. Are you still under the cloud? Did God move and you stayed put? Did you get tired of waiting on God to finally do something, so you folded up your tents and set out ahead of Him? Pray and ask God to show you where His cloud is and wait on His timing to move.

DAY #2

COMING HOME

He grew up in Christian school. He attended Church Youth Group every Wednesday and church every Sunday. Two days before his eighteenth birthday, he packed his things while his parents were at church and left. No note. No phone call. Just an empty bedroom. Gone. In the coming years, he would live in multiple states, sleeping on couches, and spending every penny of the small amount of money his mother left him before she passed away in 2009. He walked away from his family and from God. His distance from God slowly grew to disdain and then outright rebellion against Him.

He didn't just turn away from the Lord. This young man turned against Him. Then he met a girl and she became pregnant. Suddenly his world went from thinking about one person to caring for three and the young couple struggled to keep their heads above water. Committed to each other, the two young people married and focused on raising their little girl, in spite of having no real place to call home. They lived with other people, moved into a housing project, and even spent a season living in their car with their baby girl.

Finally, they found a place to live permanently. Or so they thought. Then their world again fell apart, through no fault of their own, and they found themselves looking for a place to live. But this time it was different. You see, this young man is my son. And about a year earlier, we reconciled all of our collective differences and he became one of my best friends. Before their deteriorating housing situation completely imploded, they came over a few times each week.

My wife and I encouraged my son to find a new job and he did. We knew all he really needed was one small victory to see his own potential. They moved into our house, short term, at the beginning of December. For the first time in years, we had an excited four-year-old in the house on Christmas morning. In truth, we only saw her about a dozen times over the first three years of her life, so it was a joyful time in our home. Since my son and I both work from home, we spent our days sitting across the dining room table from each other, working on our respective laptops while recovering lost years as father and son.

Six weeks after moving into our home, they found a new home in South Carolina and relocated. Honestly, even now, there's still a bit of a hole in our world because we grew accustomed to our granddaughter talking up a storm at 7:30 every morning over chocolate chip pancakes. I still miss seeing my son across the table from me but I know God has a plan. The entire time they lived under our roof, we did our best to show the love of Christ, in spite of all of the past battles.

On the final Sunday our extended family lived with us, they came to church. They'd been coming regularly but we were still always a bit shocked to get a "Yes" to our weekly invitation to join us. We drove separately to church that morning, because the kids had to say a few "Goodbyes" to other family members before heading north for the foreseeable future. On the way to church, his wife began feeling sick. The closer we got to church, the worse the nausea got. My wife and I were unaware of what was happening in the car behind us but when we arrived in the parking lot of the church, my son ran over and nearly collapsed in my arms, sobbing.

"I didn't know what to do", he said between sobs, "so I put my hand on her back and asked God to take the sickness away." Then he whispered into my ear, so as not to be heard by his wife, "She just got out of the car and said, 'I beat it,' but I know it was God." Now running late for service, we walked quickly into the building and found a place to sit. As we stood for worship, my son and his wife both sat in their seats. My son was crying. His wife leaned into him and I heard her whisper, "For the first time in a long time, I feel hope." As our pastor brought the message, which happened to be the beginning of a month-long series, the final Scripture was displayed on the screen . . .

They will be able to place their hands on the sick, and they will be healed.

Mark 16:18b NLT

I casually threw an elbow into my son, and he looked up and smiled. It was that day my son rededicated himself to Jesus. He had indeed come home. Sitting right beside him, his wife handed the Lordship of her life over to Christ. And that afternoon, instead of watching cartoons, all three of them sat on the couch and watched VeggieTales videos (on VHS tape, old school style).

My son even went to my Tuesday night men's small group. On the way through the door, I cautioned him that they may ask him to talk and I assured him I would "deflect and absorb" so he didn't need to speak. "I'll talk about everything," he commented. And believe me, he did. As he recounted every detail, he concluded with a statement I will never forget. "You know," he said, "I've done a lot of people dirty. I've done horrible things to people, stolen from them, and abandoned them without warning. I would get tired of rules and just move on to the next house, starting with his." He pointed at me as he brought his story to a close, "And the one I treated the worst is the only one who was willing to welcome me back. It didn't matter what I had done to them, they just let us move back in. My dad showed me who God really is by forgiving me and opening the house up to my family."

In the story of the Prodigal Son found in the Gospel of Luke, a young man took his inheritance, ran away from home, and squandered every penny on wild living. Once bankrupt, he decided his only option was to return home. Knowing full well his father wasn't going to be too happy with him, the son decided to appeal to his common sense. He figured if his dad fed the slaves well, he would just offer up his services as a slave, since there was zero chance he would ever been treated as a son again. The young man rehearsed his lines as he traveled back to his hometown and received a very unexpected response from his father.

But while he was still a long way off, his father saw him and was filled with compassion for him; he ran to his son, threw his arms around him and kissed him.

Luke 15:20

Nearly every time I speak to a group of men, regardless the size of the group or city they live in, at least one of them is struggling with a prodigal child. Relationships break down, kids take off, and suddenly decades are lost. Often, the catalyst creating the meltdown is long forgotten. Maybe you're in that place right now. You can't quite figure out what happened, but you miss your kid. Maybe today is the day for you to reach out to them. Go see them.

Know this. Prodigal children do come home, so get that robe and ring ready. Our job is to love them until they do. And when they do, no words need to be spoken. Just love them. God will handle the rest because He wants them back more than we do. He loves them more than we can.

Love is patient, love is kind. It does not envy, it does not boast, it is not proud. It does not dishonor others, it is not self-seeking, it is not easily angered, it keeps no record of wrongs.

1 Corinthians 13:4–5

DAY #3

MARCHING ORDERS

Has there ever been something burdening your life that just won't go away no matter how long you pray? A prayer need that seems to go perpetually unanswered? I think we've all had one or more of those at some point in life. For nearly fifteen long years, my son was a central topic of a lot of my prayers. Truth be told, probably about ninety-five percent of my prayers centered around him. Nothing I prayed to God or said to my son had any impact. And if you've ever been in a situation like that, the overwhelming temptation to give up praying altogether becomes the prevailing thought more often than not.

Joshua was a warfighter and second-in-command to Moses during the Exodus. One of the first major orders Joshua ever received from Moses involved taking a dozen spies into enemy territory to assess the viability of conquering the area. The area of operations was Canaan, also known as "The Promised Land." This roughly 60,000 square mile piece of land located on the eastern edge of the Mediterranean Sea was the ground promised by God to Abraham, Isaac, Jacob, and consequently a few hundred thousand Israelites. It was to ultimately be the permanent home of the nation of Israel, after Moses led them out of Egypt, and out of a season of slavery spanning nearly 430 years.

Of the twelve spies who went "inside the wire" to Canaan, all but two of them felt the enemy forces were far too much for their unseasoned band of homeless nomads. Sure, they'd all be given assignments in the army of Israel but they weren't exactly battle-hardened in the face of a larger opposing force. Ten of the twelve scouts returned from their recon mission into the Promised Land with some pretty daunting intelligence reports, claiming sightings of giants, fortified cities, and massive armies. Only Joshua and his battle buddy Caleb reassured Moses the whole area was an easy victory with God on point.

If you are familiar with the story of Moses and the Exodus, the second plotline involves the solemn fact Moses was to miss the Promised Land. As a result of a couple of tactical failures by the leader of Israel during their departure from Egypt, God made it clear no one from the current generation would ever set foot in the Promised Land. Everyone from the original crew of Israelite slaves would die in the desert, with the exceptions of Joshua and Caleb.

In fact, the closest Moses ever got to their new homeland was a bird's eye view from the top of a mountain on the other side of the Jordan River, where he ultimately died. After an impressive exit from Egypt and forty years of wandering in the desert, Moses died on the wrong side of the river, leaving Joshua and Caleb to lead Israel across the river and into their new homeland.

But God's plan didn't involve simply handing over all of that land adjacent to the Mediterranean. Joshua and the twelve tribes of Israel had to physically take the land over, one town at a time. And mission objective number one after crossing the Jordan was Jericho, a heavily fortified city full of combat ready warriors. In fact, word of the advancing Israelites arrived in Jericho well ahead of Joshua and his army, so the people of the walled city locked the gates. The Bible says **no one went out and no one came in** (Joshua 6:1b).

Needless to say, Joshua likely assumed the attack on Jericho would be tactically similar to every other successful Israelite campaign—just kick down the door, kill everyone and take over. But God had a completely different tactic for the Battle of Jericho:

Then the Lord said to Joshua, "See, I have delivered Jericho into your hands, along with its king and its fighting men. March around the city once with all the armed men. Do this for six days. Have seven priests carry trumpets of rams' horns in front of the ark. On the seventh day, march around the city seven times, with the priests blowing the trumpets. When you hear them sound a long blast on the trumpets, have the whole army give a loud shout; then the wall of the city will collapse and the army will go up, everyone straight in."

Joshua 6:3–5

Essentially, this newly appointed leader of the army of Israel had to tell his roughly 40,000 soldiers they were to march around the city once a day. That's all. Just get up, go to the rally point outside the city, and walk around the nearly fifty-foot-high wall encompassing Jericho. Then go back to camp and wait for the next day's trip around the walls.

Remembering this generation of soldiers did not see miracles like the parting of the Red Sea as their parent's had, some of them had to be seriously doubting Joshua's prowess as a commander. They committed to Moses, prior to his death, they would faithfully serve Joshua just as they had Moses. But they had to be thinking Joshua had lost his mind with this plan.

And Joshua may have been a little overwhelmed also. He had a heart of obedience to the Lord and knew God was a God of His word but he was leading a lot of soldiers who may not have had the same level of faith. Let's just assume there may have been a little grumbling over leadership within the rank and file a few times over that week outside Jericho. But the rest is history.

When the trumpets sounded, the army shouted, and at the sound of the trumpet, when the men gave a loud shout, the wall collapsed; so everyone charged straight in, and they took the city.

Joshua 6:20

As is His nature, God did precisely as He said He would, and the walls around Jericho came crashing to the ground.

Think about that week of camping and walking, camping and walking, and camping and walking. Every morning, the soldiers' only assignment was to walk the half mile perimeter of Jericho and return to base camp, all the while hoping the promise of day seven would result in a victory.

Can you imagine what would have happened had Joshua quit the mission on day six? "Forget this," he could have said, "This is clearly not going to happen. I give up." Jericho would still be standing, the nation of Israel would have moved on to the next town, and one of the greatest victories in conquest of the Promised Land would never have happened. But Joshua stuck to the plan and did exactly what God told him to do and God gave them victory.

Is there a battle going on in your life right now going unresolved no matter how much you pray? Did you give up before God answered? God may be up in Heaven today saying, "All I need you to do is pray for one more day. Just one more day." The last thing we want to do is give up one day before the miracle.

Today is the day to arise and walk around your Jericho yet again. Maybe you quit one day before the walls were going to come down. All it was going to take was one more lap around the problem. Trust God to bring you a victory today. The walls will come down.

DAY #4

WORDS MATTER

I spent the half hour drive to the restaurant running through my internal script. We decided to meet halfway between our two houses to finally address the elephant in our relational living room. My twenty-three-year-old son, Jordan, agreed to meet with me, primarily to deal with the root of years of interpersonal struggle. We had been "off and on" for over a decade, with great holiday seasons interspersed with long seasons of very pronounced absences. The only real problem was determining what "the root of the struggle" truly was.

Formulating my own conclusion about the aforementioned root some years earlier, I had my speech all prepared as we walked into the restaurant. Having watched my son's interactions and listened to his words over the past decade, it was blatantly obvious the root of our problems revolved around his stepmother, my wife, Joni. After all, his mother all but cursed Joni and me countless times, going so far as to tell my son, "You can't ever love that woman."

My ex-wife operated under the constant fear she was going to somehow be replaced as "Mom," in spite of our constant reassurances she was always "Mom." My wife was "Stepmom," and had three of her own children and certainly didn't need any more kids. I truly believe, right up until she lost her battle with cancer in 2009, my ex-wife was mortified at the mere thought of losing her children and defended that position accordingly.

I kicked off the lunchtime conversation with a self-assured defense of my wife, "You know, Joni really loves you. She never wanted to be your mother. You will always only have one mom, even though she's gone. And your stepmom—"

"Dad, dad, stop!" Jordan interrupted me, "I love Joni. That woman treated me like solid gold, even when I treated her like dirt." He continued, "I don't have a problem with her. I have a problem with YOU!"

I was dumbfounded. "Me?" I thought as I began a mental inventory of less-than-stellar dad moments. Nothing really jumped out at me. "You don't remember, do you?" he inquired as he stared directly into my face. As I shook my head and stared blankly at my son, he reminded me of something I had long forgotten. "It was a Wednesday, I was eight years old," he started, "and it was your day. Remember, you had us every other weekend and on Wednesdays overnight? Well, it was your day but I didn't want to be at your house. I wanted to be at Mom's. I was in my room, sitting on my bed playing a GameBoy game when you stood in the doorway and I told you I wanted to go back to Mom's. And you got so mad."

By now, I was just listening intently to my son's vivid and detailed recount of that Wednesday night I'd long since forgotten. "You called me a bunch of names like 'Mama's boy' and you told me to 'man up,'" he concluded, "and I will never forget that because it hurt so bad." Tears streamed down my cheeks as Jordan recalled, in vivid detail, every word I said. It was as if he was telling a story about two different men, because none of it was familiar; yet, it was believable and, at that point in my life, anything was likely to come out of my mouth. "Jordan,"

I replied, "I don't blame you for hating me. Had I said those words to myself, I wouldn't talk to me either. I am so sorry I ever said anything like that to you and I hope you can forgive me someday."

Truth be told, I wasn't even mad at little Jordan on that fateful Wednesday many years ago. I was upset at his mother for never "having my back," or for reassuring my son that every little boy needs his father. It really wasn't her fault she didn't defend me, considering she grew up without a father. In my anger at his mother, I threw verbal rocks at my little boy. And the resulting emotional injury lasted over fifteen years.

Words hurt. And whether we can remember, often the other party can not only remember words but even the setting and circumstances. The Bible makes it very clear just how powerful our words can be in a number of different verses. Today, I would ask you truly meditate on the following Scripture verses, while you allow God to reveal to you any wounding words you may have spoken to someone else.

The tongue has the power of life and death

Proverbs 18:21a

Do not let any unwholesome talk come out of your mouths, but only what is helpful for building others up according to their needs, that it may benefit those who listen.

Ephesians 4:29

Gentle words are a tree of life; a deceitful tongue crushes the spirit.

Proverbs 15:4 NLT

There is one whose rash words are like sword thrusts.

Proverbs 12:18a ESV

Do you see a man who is hasty in his words? There is more hope for a fool than for him.

Proverbs 29:20 ESV

As you go through this week, do an inventory of your spouse, kids, and even co-workers or employees. Ask them one simple question, "Have I ever said anything to you that hurt your feelings?" If you get a "Yes," don't defend it and don't make excuses. Simply tell them "I can see how that would hurt" and then look them in the eye and ask forgiveness. You never know who is hanging on to painful words we've spoken and the freedom of working through those verbal wounds can often open the door to relational restoration and reconciliation. Don't wait. Do it today.

DAY #5

OUR OWN WORST ENEMY

I spent much of the early 2000's as salesperson for a home-builder. Being in the retirement capital of the world, South-west Florida, I was very busy selling homes to people from all over the Midwest, who'd driven down to find their utopian piece of retirement heaven. Then, in 2005, as if someone slammed the entrance gates to the state of Florida closed, all of the traffic into my model home virtually stopped. Without explanation, my days shifted from frantically running from home to home in various states of construction to sitting at my desk just hoping one person would walk through the door in any given week.

But, while my model home may have been devoid of sales prospects, this was a season in my life where God immersed me in His Word. The extent of my eight hours each day consisted almost exclusively of turning on the model's lights, then reading the Word all day, then shutting down the lights at the close of business. And it was during this same season God called me into ministry to men, which, in hindsight, was absolutely nuts. My wife confirmed it many times in the past, but I felt now was finally the time. I shared the vision with my boss the following day and he gave me his blessing. In fact, he has been my accountability partner since that day.

The logical next step in my journey toward ministry was to speak to my pastor about it, as he was my spiritual authority. "You're not going to make it," he cautioned me over lunch, "because you don't have a degree and you really need to provide for your family. The Bible says if a man doesn't work, he doesn't eat. How about leading a small group at church instead?" While I struggled to digest my pastor's words, I still felt as though I was truly called.

Pursuing confirmation, I sought the input of a well-known men's ministry author I'd been indirectly working for over the previous few months. "You'll never make it without a book or a nest egg, David," he explained to me, "No one has ever made men's ministry a career without a pulpit or a book. No one will support it as a standalone ministry."

Defeated, I drove home from that meeting second-guessing myself. And second-guessing God. "Maybe they're right," I thought to myself, "I don't have a theology degree, a book or any support." On top of all of that, the deteriorating real estate market all but consumed every dime I'd earned, and we were, in fact, financially upside-down. We went so far as to use credit cards to pay bills, praying for the market to turn so we could begin the process of righting our personal financial shipwreck.

In the Book of Judges in the Old Testament, we meet a young man named Gideon. His story doesn't take up more than about a chapter and half of Judges, but it becomes evident very quickly God doesn't call the equipped; but rather, He equips those whom He has called. Gideon was just a young man who spent his days threshing wheat hidden inside a winepress to prevent the enemy, the Midianites, from discovering their food supply. At this point in Biblical history, the Midianites have managed to overwhelm Israel, so much so their survival was in question. So, the Israelites cry out to God and He sets apart a man to deliver them from Midianite oppression.

One day, Gideon is doing his usual job when an angel of the LORD shows up and says, "The Lord is with you, mighty warrior." Like most of us "average Joes with average jobs," being called a warrior wasn't exactly the self-image young Gideon had of himself.

As promised, God was raising up a warrior to deliver Israel from the Midianites. And that warrior was Gideon. However, Gideon didn't exactly see it working out too well, given his pronounced lack of anything even remotely resembling a warrior.

The Lord turned to him and said, "Go in the strength you have and save Israel out of Midian's hand. Am I not sending you?"

"Pardon me, my lord," Gideon replied, "but how can I save Israel? My clan is the weakest in Manasseh, and I am the least in my family."

The Lord answered, "I will be with you, and you will strike down all the Midianites, leaving none alive."

Judges 6:14–16

Needless to say, Gideon's reply was based on how he viewed himself, not how God saw him. God saw a job needing to be done and He assigned that task to Gideon. If you're familiar with the rest of the story, not only was Gideon the smallest guy from the smallest tribe, but his vision of what was needed to complete God's mission was well beyond what God needed. In Judges 7, the newly-appointed leader rallies 30,000 men to attack Midian, which God immediately classifies as "too many men" (v2). So, God thins the ranks by 20,000, leaving Gideon only a third of his original fighting force.

But the Lord said to Gideon, "There are still too many men."

Judges 7:4a

At this point, Gideon has got to be losing his mind. Thirty thousand was too many. Twenty thousand was too many. So God ultimately drew down Gideon's forces to a whopping 300 men. The 300 end up broken into three 100-man detachments, armed with nothing more that trumpets and empty jars with torches inside them, to confront an opposing force the Bible says were "thick as locusts" and their "camels could no more be counted than the sand on the seashore." (v12)

At the onset of the battle, the men blew the trumpets, broke the jars, and the enemy turned on each other, resulting in a resounding victory without a "shot fired," so to speak. God used a no-name wheat thresher from the smallest tribe in Israel to defeat over 100,000 Midianites and rescue Israel from certain eradiation.

Thankfully, after fifteen years and God opening some crazy doors, we are still in ministry. Don't get me wrong; there is wisdom in a multitude of counselors (Proverbs 15:22). But God asks the most unlikely people to accomplish His work, as we see in the people like Moses, Joseph, and even a donkey (Numbers 22).

Has God burdened your heart with a mission difficult to even comprehend? Have you been overthinking a calling, because you're under-qualified, under-educated or have a past that just doesn't equate to being an instrument for God?

Maybe it's time to quiet the voice of your own worst critic—yourself. Listen to the marching orders of the Holy Spirit and pursue that calling. He's given you the vision to see the mission and He won't let you down when it comes to the power to execute it. Ask God to show you the next step to fully respond to the sound of His calling on your life. He has called you for a time such as this and you are the right person for the job.

DAY #6

SPIRITUAL LEADERSHIP

Growing up without God or a church, or a relationship with Jesus, I ultimately met the Lord in my mid-thirties after losing a marriage, my home, and my kids. God often reaches men through crisis, and I'm no different. He meets us on our ground, often after we've leveled that ground with a relational bomb blast or a financial landmine. There's a lot of truth to the old adage: "You don't know how much you need Jesus until Jesus is all you've got." Many men find themselves at a breaking point and often there's collateral damage in our families as well. But God can often use those moments to transform a man as well as those around him.

In my devotional time this morning, I ran across one of those stories in the Bible I've blown past at least a dozen times. But today, God revealed something that resonated with me as a man of God, a father, and a husband. This particular recount follows several other, more prominent stories in the Gospel of John, chapter 4. Here's a brief backstory. Shortly after meeting the Samaritan woman at the well, there is a revival in Samaria, where "many Samaritans believed" (John

4:39). After staying in the area for another couple of days, Jesus and His disciples strike out for Galilee, which is Jesus's hometown. Surprisingly, although Jesus mentioned a "prophet has no honor in His own country" (v44), the Galileans welcomed Him with open arms, primarily due to the fact they heard about the Samarian revival.

Jesus finds Himself back in lower Galilee, in an area known as Cana, where He performed His first recorded miracle of turning water into wine. This is where we meet an official, whose son is sick and about seventeen miles away in Capernaum. When the official heard Jesus was in town, he went to Him, and begged Jesus to heal his sick son.

"Unless you people see signs and wonders," Jesus told him, "you will never believe."

The royal official said, "Sir, come down before my child dies."

"Go," Jesus replied, "your son will live."

The man took Jesus at his word and departed. While he was still on the way, his servants met him with the news that his boy was living. When he inquired as to the time when his son got better, they said to him, "Yesterday, at one in the afternoon, the fever left him."

John 4:48–52

Honestly, this story is quite similar to ones we've read before, whether it be the Roman centurion's servant seen in Matthew 8:5–13 or Jairus's daughter in Matthew 9:18–26. Jesus proves on multiple occasions He needn't be in the vicinity of a sick (or dead) person to still have an impact. The royal official just asked for his own personal miracle and Jesus made His son well. But that's not the part of John 4 that really jumped off the page at me. This is:

Then the father realized that this was the exact time at which Jesus had said to him, "Your son will live." So he and his whole household believed.

John 4:53

Clearly it took some time to cover the nearly twenty-mile trip from Cana to Capernaum and the servants intercepted the royal official on the way home to give him the news of his son's healing. The official wasn't home when his son's fever broke, but when he heard the news, he immediately believed. I'd like to think he believed before the healing, as he had just enough faith to find Jesus in Cana and beg for a healing. And as a result of his faith in asking for a healing, his whole household also believed.

I'll never forget the moment, back in 2003, when my wife and I sat on our bed with my son and my daughter as they both accepted Jesus as their Lord and Savior. Granted, there have been a lot of bumps along the way but both my kids have found God on their own terms. Had Jesus not grabbed my heart first, neither of them would likely even know who Jesus is today. As Joshua spoke in Joshua 24:15, "As for me and my household, we will serve the Lord." My wife, children, and stepkids all know Who we serve in our house, thanks to God going after this broken man in the middle of an epic crisis.

As the spiritual leaders of our homes, we men have the responsibility to lead. And wherever men lead, more often than not, the family will follow. Evangelist DL Moody once wrote, "A man ought to live so that everybody knows he is a Christian... and most of all, his family ought to know." My wife once mentioned to me, when I'm up early doing my quiet time, she feels like I'm in a tower providing overwatch for the entire family.

Here's the hard question: Where are you leading today? Are they seeing you in the Word? Do they know, when challenges arise, God is your first line of offense? Are you praying over your spouse and kids every day? No, I don't mean the cursory pre-dinner kick off prayer. I mean face down prayers for their health, their walks with Jesus, their future spouses, and Godly friends.

If not, start today. You have been given authority, by Jesus, over your entire household. And wherever you lead, they will follow. Pray God shows you your strengths—and weaknesses—as a leader. Ask Him to ramp up your personal spiritual disciplines, so it truly models Godly leadership to the next generation. They are watching us lead. It's up to us where we lead them.

DAY #7

THE BALANCE OF
WORK AND HOME

alk the Line is one of my all-time favorite movies. The winner of five Academy Awards, including "Best Actor" and "Best Actress," the film is a pseudo-biographical account of legendary country music singer, Johnny Cash. After a struggle for his musical identity during his early life, Johnny finally finds his musical "sweet spot" a few years after marrying his long-time girlfriend, Vivian. As his career escalates to national fame, Cash finds himself on a near-endless county fair tour with the likes of musical legends Jerry Lee Lewis, Elvis Pressley, and Roy Orbison.

Returning from months on the road, Johnny arrives home for a well-deserved break. The Cash's now live in a much larger home, more suitable for a famous musician than their previous little apartment in Nashville. Clearly, Johnny is making some money, so he outfits the home with everything a growing family needs. But there's a very pronounced piece missing.

While making dinner for the family, Vivian loses track of her road-weary husband. As it happens, Johnny is sound asleep in a chair in another room. Frustrated her husband has checked out of the family already, she walks into the room and simply says, "Better start living life here with us when you come home, before you have to leave again."

Johnny's deflects the statement by talking about their most recent tour escapades, which only seems to widen the gap between the man and his wife. Vivian responds by putting a stop to any future tour talk while Johnny is home, which her husband simply can't understand. Johnny protests having rules at home and honestly can't understand why Vivian doesn't appreciate the big dream house filled with "all the pretty little things" they've ever needed. Her glaring reply is similar to one echoed by many wives, "I want you, John, I want you! And I want everything that you promised to me."

Sometimes balancing work and family can be a struggle. But God makes it clear our front-line ministry—our family—should always be a priority. And it all starts with our marriage:

In the same way husbands should love their wives as their own bodies. He who loves his wife loves himself. For no one ever hated his own flesh, but nourishes and cherishes it, just as Christ does the church, because we are members of his body.

Ephesians 4:28–30

Our children fall next in line under our wives and need to know they are also important. In the Old Testament, Moses encourages us to spend time with our children, speaking of the things of God. Remember, kids spell love, t-i-m-e and *God IS love* (1 John 4:8b).

Love the Lord your God with all your heart and with all your soul and with all your strength. These commandments that I give you today are to be on your hearts. Impress them on your children.

Talk about them when you sit at home and when you walk along the road, when you lie down and when you get up.

Deuteronomy 6:5–7

When I was a young father, I had a dream to become a professional bowler. I spent a lot of time at the bowling alley on my lunch breaks and bowled in a competitive three-man "scratch" league on Wednesday nights from 9:00 p.m. until around midnight. Now, while 9:00 p.m. was well past my little boy's bed time, he was acutely aware I wasn't home.

When we had free time as a family, we would often go bowling. But truthfully, we were just doing what I wanted, and the wife and kids were simply going along for the ride. Many years later, in a somewhat heated discussion, my then-teenage son blurted out "You were never home. All you ever did was bowl all the time." In my defense, it was only during my lunch breaks at work and once per week at night, but from my boy's perspective, I sacrificed my relationship with him on the altar of bowling. His perception, likely even still, is my reality.

Have you let life throw things off balance? Has marriage taken a back seat to providing for the family? Or have personal goals trumped spending time with the kids? This devotion has two objectives, and one of them is actually pretty intimidating. First, pray God reveals any potential imbalance with regard to time, work, hobbies, and family. Second, if we really want to know the reality of our day-to-day decisions, we must ask those inside the wire at our home HQ. Ask your wife, "Is there something I can be doing better as a husband?" and ask your kids, "How can I be a better dad?" True humility as a man of God involves asking the hard questions and occasionally hearing even harder answers.

As a father of adult children who've gone on to begin their own married lives, I only wish someone had cautioned me about the possible collateral damage of my workaholism and my passion for bowling.

Follow the prompting of the Holy Spirit today and make adjustments accordingly. Today could change your marriage, your children, and the generations after you.

DAY #8

FACING THE WORLD

Daniel is one of my favorite Bible heroes, mostly because of his steadfast resolve to honor God no matter the cost. We first meet him, as one would expect, in the book in the Bible by the same name. Daniel is a book packed with powerful examples of full-throttle faith in the Lord. Honestly, sometimes I feel like I'd be invincible if I had just the faith in Daniel's pinky finger. This guy is legend.

Raised as Jewish nobility in a rapidly deteriorating nation of Israel (this primarily due to years of overt disobedience to God), young Daniel and three of his buddies, Hananiah, Mishael, and Azariah are carried off to Babylon. Needless to say, by this point in biblical history, Jerusalem has been conquered by King Nebuchadnezzar and the Babylonians, and most of the nation of Israel has either been killed off or hauled off.

Because of their physical stature, appearance, and obvious intelligence, Daniel and his friends are taken to Babylon to serve in the court of the King. Their assignment was to learn the language, food, and culture of the Babylonians in order to best serve the leadership of their new, albeit temporary, "homeland." The young men are afforded the best of everything the culture had to offer, including food from the king's own personal chef. They even get new names for their new "lives": Daniel was named Belteshazzar, Hananiah became Shadrach, Mishael was given the name Meshach, and Azariah was called Abednego.

Imagine what "the best of everything" would look like in today's culture—"Daniel, we are taking you and your three friends to Babylon, where you will live in a Park Avenue penthouse, eat five-star food every day, have access to the best gym, and carry the best iPhones."

These young men were most likely teenagers when they were relocated to Babylon, which would have made the appeal of the aforementioned "best of everything" hard to resist. While in Jerusalem, they were probably living in horrid conditions after Babylon all but vaporized their city. They may have even gone hungry a few times after the supply lines to Israel were cut off by the enemy. Then they're offered the best food money can buy and kingdom-caliber living arrangements. Yet these four young men, led by Daniel, make a pivotal and counter-cultural decision to go against what was expected of new kingdom "recruits."

But Daniel resolved not to defile himself with the royal food and wine, and he asked the chief official for permission not to defile himself this way.

Daniel 1:8

Contrary to the others, Daniel and his friends stand against the prevailing culture by refusing to eat their special food, instead requesting a menu consisting of nothing more than vegetables and water. Needless to say, the official appointed over the young men was hesitant but God gave them favor in the eyes of the official and he agreed. All Daniel requested was a simple physical comparison between his team and the other recruits, who would be eating the royal food. If their diet backfired, Daniel agreed to eat like the other guys.

At the end of the ten days they looked healthier and better nourished than any of the young men who ate the royal food.

Daniel 1:15

Their collective decision to go against the grain of the culture resulted in a resounding victory for Daniel and his three teammates. They ended up in better physical condition by choosing a different path. Interestingly, although Daniel was given a new name when he arrived in Babylon, the Bible continues to use his Hebrew name throughout the book of Daniel. Daniel never succumbed to the culture of the world.

The culture of the world today has incredible pull on believers and non-believers alike. Turn on the television and you'll be bombarded with better cars, the latest tech, the diet-trend-of-the-week, and clothes and hair color to can make us look younger. Add to that the incessant barrage of worldly enticement dangled in front of us via social media. If we aren't vigilant, a single compromise can destroy our entire legacy. Compromise is like trying to walk down a steep, muddy hill. The first step can be challenging to keep our balance but the rest of the way down that hill is fast and easy.

If you're familiar with the rest of the story of Daniel, not only do these four trainees opt for a different diet. They ultimately stand their ground again on something far more important—bowing to a false god.

Another part of their initiation into Babylon involved honoring King Nebuchadnezzar's recently constructed statue. Clearly this is a violation of the original Ten Commandments, so Daniel, Shadrach, Meshach, and Abednego flatly refuse. To make them an example to the others, the king orders them thrown into a fire, and even facing certain destruction, Daniel and his fireteam never falter. And God delivers the men from death by walking through the fire with them. Most importantly, others were watching, and God was glorified.

Standing our ground in a world constantly pressing us to conform requires discipline. And a team. We need men around us to fight the battle.

Every fireteam has a leader. He's the guy who knows the area of operations and the mission. Daniel was that guy. He resolved not to defile himself, whether it be from food or idol worship. This young Hebrew was willing to pay the price of his unwavering faith in God and his three friends were well aware of where Daniel stood. And they stood with him, no matter the cost. Solomon said it best:

Though one may be overpowered, two can defend themselves.

Ecclesiastes 4:12a

Where have you seen the world slowly encroach on your walk with the Lord? Is there something you've been pursuing that resembles a modern-day Babylon? Ask God to show you where the things or the cares of the world have built a stronghold in your heart. Share what He shows you with your battle buddies and ask them to pray against potential breaches in your spiritual defenses.

Set your minds on things above, not on earthly things.

Colossians 3:2

DAY #9

EXCEEDINGLY, ABUNDANTLY

During the eighteen-month filming process of our location-based *Who Has Your Six* video series, my wife and our team found ourselves in amazing places like Omaha Beach in France, on Doughboy Football Field at Fort Benning, and even the gameday locker room at the University of Notre Dame. Everywhere we landed, God showed up in a big way, giving us favor to film in places we should have never been allowed, and connecting us to the right people to make each video happen just the way I'd envisioned. And this particular shoot was going to be no different because God was always right there in our midst.

Excitedly, we packed the car for the eight-hour drive to Bayou la Batre, Alabama, the shrimp capital of the world. After all, if you're going to film a *Forrest Gump* segment, why not go to the home of Benjamin Buford Blue, aka "Bubba?" Only this time was a little different. I had no plan and no point of contact, other than a pin stuck in a map. As we neared the location, my wife asked me a terrifying question: "Okay, we are almost there, so what's our plan?" Oops. I had forgotten to mention my lack of a plan, so my response was something like "Well, I don't have a point of contact, so here's what we are going to do. We are going to drive into Bayou la Batre, find some shrimp boats and film there." While our producer cackled at me from the back seat, my wife flatly replied, "That's your plan? That's a horrible plan."

Well, it was too late to turn back. I'd never even been to Bayou la Batre, so I honestly didn't know if they even had shrimp boats. As we pulled into the little Alabama bayou town, I was relieved to see boat rigging towering behind countless warehouses. The town oddly resembled Venice, Italy, with canals full of shrimp boats down every street. We passed dozens of warehouses, looking for a viable dock with some boats in the background. I originally wanted to film in the town square in Savannah, Georgia, but I discovered the bench was a prop, as was Forrest's home in the factitious town of "Greenbow, Alabama." So Bayou la Batre was all I had left.

"That's a good one," I said pointing toward a huge warehouse with a perfect dock behind it. On the other side of the inlet from the dock were eight colorful shrimp boats—the perfect backdrop. After searching for an hour, we found our spot. Given that we didn't want to arbitrarily set up camera gear on some guy's dock, our producer, Ryan, and I decided to ask permission. We knocked on the portable trailer in front of the warehouse, and a faint "Come in" could be heard. As we opened the door, Ryan said "Remember what God has done so far with these shoots. This is going to be better than we think."

Immediately, I was faced by a woman. A seemingly not-so-happy sort, smoking a cigarette behind her cluttered desk. I proceeded to introduce myself, stated we were creating a video series for the U.S. Army, mentioned the connection to the movie *Forrest Gump*, and asked permission to shoot on their dock.

"It's not my dock," she glared at me. "It's not?" I asked, completely baffled given the fact it was literally directly behind their warehouse. "No, it's Dominick's dock." That was the name on the big sign on the warehouse: "Dominick's Seafood Company." I was a little nervous at that point but asked, "Do you happen to know where we would find Dominick?" From behind the door, I heard a muffled "I'm right here." Evidently, when we opened the trailer door, Dominick was behind it.

Dominick stood and with an emotionless facial expression, extended a hand to silently introduce himself. Then he beamed a huge smile, "Buddy, I heard everything you said. You're welcome to use my dock for anything you need. I even have a sixty-footer (a shrimp boat) you can film on if you'd like." He concluded with, "But, before you do any filming, there's someone I want you to meet. Follow me."

At that point, we have no idea where we are going but we obediently follow the captain down the trailer hall to a little office. Dominick introduced us to his first mate, Mike. "You guys have something in common," Dominick stated as he walked back to the front of the office.

As I shook Mike's hand, sizing him up and realizing we had exactly nothing in common, God again showed up. "So, you like *Forrest Gump*? What a great movie," Mike said with a smile, "I was the technical consultant for all the shrimp boat scenes for *Forrest Gump*. I showed Tom Hanks how to run the ropes and drive the boat."

Ryan and I stood there with our jaws on the floor. We passed at least fifty warehouses by the time we got to Dominick. And the guy who helped make the movie we were basing our filming on was inside the trailer God led us to. Out of the eight videos we created, Bayou la Batre is still one of my absolute favorites. We saw God take a vision I had and bring it to completion even better than I imagined.

I wanted to use today's devotional to share that story because what God has birthed in you isn't done yet. God isn't done with your dream, even if it looks like that dream is flat-line dead. He's still on the throne and organizing the outcome, but it's on His timing. That's a hard one for me sometimes, because I just want it done and am not good at waiting. Remember . . .

. . . being confident of this, that he who began a good work in you will carry it on to completion until the day of Christ Jesus.

Philippians 1:6

I've lived the personal struggle over and over. It's not happening fast enough or the way I imagined it. So today, press into Him, expecting nothing but His presence and His peace in your life. My wife continually reminds me it's all about our vertical walk, not the horizontal one. In other words, it's all about our daily relationship with God. If we focus on that vertical walk with the Lord, He will handle the horizontal logistics of our relationships, our marriages, our businesses, and our children.

Delight yourself in the LORD, and he will give you the desires of your heart.

Psalm 37:4

And as can be seen by my trip to the Alabama bayou, He doesn't just "handle the horizontal logistics." If we press into Him, God will provide beyond our wildest dreams.

Now to Him who is able to do exceedingly abundantly above all that we ask or think, according to the power that works in us, to Him be glory in the church by Christ Jesus to all generations, forever and ever. Amen.

Ephesians 3:20–21

Have you let go of a dream because it's just too overwhelming? Is there a relationship that appears unrecoverable? Maybe it's an endless job search or a prodigal child who never calls back. Seek God's face and tell Him the desires of your heart and let Him put the right pieces in the right places. In Jesus's name.

DAY #10

STRONGER
THAN OAK

Throughout my life as a believer in Christ and as an unbeliever, I've dealt with a lot of different people. I've been a manager of hundreds, a sales consultant to quirky and demanding people who are building their very first home, and even a coach to five-year-old soccer players—complete with the fathers and mothers of those players. And along the way, I've heard it all, seen it all, and probably said it all, too.

Not a week goes by without something reminding me of a scene from *Jerry Maguire*, that Tom Cruise movie about the professional sports agent who makes a living recruiting top college prospects and managing a litany of professional athletes. After starting his own agency, he's left with exactly one prospect—a college quarterback named Frank Cushman, who's being recruited by every NFL team and every agent.

Jerry has him on the hook as the front-runner in the agent race. The only challenge is the prospect's father, played by Beau Bridges, won't sign a contract for representation. While he won't sign anything, the athlete's father assures Jerry, "My word is my bond. I don't sign contracts, but what you do have is my whole word, and it's stronger than oak." Consequently, Maguire and Cushman's dad seal the deal with a firm handshake.

Even if you haven't seen *Jerry Maguire*, you can probably guess what happens next. Another agent, the unethical Bob Sugar, comes in and steals the contract from Jerry, and even gets it in writing. It's NFL signing day and Sugar has just stolen Maguire's biggest client. Angered by being dumped, Jerry confronts the young quarterback's father saying, "I'm still sort of moved by your 'stronger than oak' thing." But no deal. Jerry's out and Sugar's in.

"My word is stronger than oak." You know, an oak is a big tree and its wood is incredibly dense, immensely durable, and one of the strongest woods in existence. To give you an idea of just how durable an oak tree can be, the Bowthorpe Oak tree in England is estimated to be around a thousand years old. Craftsmen make wine barrels, floors, and even Viking ships out of oak. So to see something that strong compromised in any way would take a whole lot of force. Unless, that is, it wasn't made of oak in the first place.

As men of God, our word should truly be our bond. It should be as strong as the Bowthorpe Oak and just as enduring. The Bible is really clear about how important our word is, in both the Old Testament and the New Testament.

But whoever keeps His word, truly the love of God is perfected in him. By this we know that we are in Him.

1 John 2:5 NKJV

But let your 'Yes' be 'Yes,' and your 'No,' 'No.' For whatever is more than these is from the evil one.

Matthew 5:37 NKJV

Often, the ones closest to us are the people who deal with our words being made more like a balsa wood airplane than a Viking ship. "Something has come up" is one of the most painful phrases a child can hear while waiting for Dad to show up at a recital or a ball game. The words "Maybe we can do it next week" can hurt our wives more than we realize, as they wait for us to get home from work for date night.

If a man makes a vow to the Lord, or swears an oath to bind himself by some agreement, he shall not break his word; he shall do according to all that proceeds out of his mouth.

Numbers 30:2 NKJV

If you're like me, you've probably failed a commitment or two. The good news is it's never too late to apologize for missing an important function. Seeking forgiveness from our wife or our kid is the first step to moving forward.

The second step is making sure we don't let it happen again, by subscribing to the following tactics:

- If you say you're going to do something, do it
- If you commit to following through with a task, do it. On time
- If you make a commitment to faithfully love your wife until death, do it
- If you tell your kid you'll be at his game, recital or practice, be there
- If you set an appointment to call or meet, keep it
- If you screw something up, relationally or even physically, own it
- If you have to re-schedule, do it in advance, not as an apology after the fact.

This isn't just because being a man of integrity requires the aforementioned but keep in mind other people (aka- your sons, daughters, co-workers, etc.) are going to follow our lead. If it's okay for us then it's okay for them.

I'm actually somewhat weary of living in a society where making excuses and shifting the blame to someone else has become the new "normal." The root word of "commitment" is "commit" and I didn't even need a Greek or Hebrew translation to see it. When we commit, it's a covenant to follow though. It's non-negotiable and irrevocable.

As a Christian man, I am committed to living as if you could build a ship out of my word. It won't sink if you rely on it. It won't even leak. I may fail at a lot of Godly man tests but my word IS stronger than oak.

Ask God to reveal to you any past scheduling issues that may have inadvertently created a chasm between you and your family. Go to them, own it, and seek forgiveness. Pray for His leading as you speak to them.

And remember . . .

Whatever your lips utter you must be sure to do, because you made your vow freely to the LORD your God with your own mouth.

Deuteronomy 23:23

DAY #11

FINISHING WELL

Producing the *Who Has Your Six* video series was foreign territory for me. I'd never been on camera, other than the occasional TV interview. I was, in fact, completely intimidated by speaking into a camera. Along the way, I learned a lot of new industry jargon and technical terms like "Interview portion" (where I spoke into a fixed mount camera from a single location), "White balance" (adjusting the color of the picture) and "B-roll." For you non-filmmakers like me, "B-roll" is what you see on the screen while the narrator is speaking over it. It can take hours to shoot B-roll which, in some instances, will only be on the screen for a matter of seconds. For example, the cameraman would put me on a sidewalk and film my shoes as I walked. First from the front, then from the back, then from the sides, then from behind my head, and so on. Over and over again.

So, when we found ourselves on Omaha Beach in Normandy, France, to film the *Saving Private Ryan* piece, I was certain shooting the B-roll would be nothing short of a marathon. I did a lot of walking for that one—on the beach, atop the cliffside Nazi bunkers, through the streets of Colleville sur Mer, and all over the American cemetery. But the walking wasn't the hardest part. It was kneeling in front of one of the 9,387 tombstones in the cemetery that proved to be both physically, and emotionally, demanding.

"Okay," the videographer said as he pointed down the row of stones, "just kneel in front of that cross over there." In case you were wondering, kneeling for twenty minutes without falling over can be rough, especially when you have "over fifty" knees. I would hear him behind me, then catch a glance of him out of my peripheral vision manhandling that giant gyro-camera assembly. He'd zoom into my face, then literally fly it over my head. And all I did, the entire time, was stare at this soldier's name on the tombstone. He died on Omaha Beach on D-Day, June 6, 1944, about 500 meters down a cliff from where I was kneeling.

Something really hit me as I stared blankly into the cross-shaped marble. It was the formatting. Every one of those nearly 10,000 tombstones has the same information on it. On each stone, you'll first see the soldier's name, then his rank and unit below that, and finally the state he lived in, and the date he died in combat.

Ironically, one piece of information generally found on a tombstone is absent on every memorial stone in Normandy—a birth date.

You know, I have no idea how old that soldier was when he died. Was he an eighteen-year-old kid who happened to be "1A" in the draft and just ended up on that beach? Or was he a thirty-two-year-old mechanic who decided to join the fight after reading about Pearl Harbor? Or perhaps he was a twenty-eight-year-old Jewish doctor who finally had enough of seeing his people systematically slaughtered. He could have been any age, from any walk of life, and with any background.

I believe deep in the heart of every man is the desire to finish well. We are wired up to finish strong. It's in our DNA. No matter how we start, God pushes the reset button every day, giving us a new beginning. Lamentations 3:22–23 says it like this:

The steadfast love of the Lord never ceases; his mercies never come to an end; they are new every morning; great is your faithfulness.

I know I've had days when I feel like I just keep getting buried deeper. You may feel like an epic failure right now. Maybe you said the wrong thing to your kid, or your spouse. Maybe your company just folded and you're out of a job. Or perhaps you've fallen into that same old sin trap—again.

But know this and take heart: Today is a new day. Yesterday is history. It doesn't matter how you started. It only matters how you finish. The Apostle Paul emboldens us with his words to the people of Philippi:

But one thing I do: Forgetting what is behind and straining toward what is ahead, I press on toward the goal to win the prize for which God has called me heavenward in Christ Jesus.

Philippians 3:13–14

So get up, brush the dirt off, and get back in the fight.

Do you realize, apart from what's written in the marble, we know very little about the soldiers in that hilltop field in France? Were they kids? Did they have kids? Were they good fathers? Good husbands? Were some of them divorced and remarried? Alcoholics? Sunday school teachers? Business success stories or totally unemployed? Were they good guys or bad guys in their families, towns, and marketplaces?

Here's the only thing we do know. It doesn't matter what their lives were like prior to June 6, 1944. Regardless of how each of those 9,387 men lived their lives prior to the war, the only thing that matters is what happened on that solitary date found permanently etched on that French marble headstone.

Each of those men died as a war hero.

Every one of those men finished well. We should too.

DAY #12

THE FACE OFF

He was in the bathroom shaving when I decided to let him have it. "You're such a poser, dude." He looked back at me, in shock, with a blank "What do you mean?" stare. "You call yourself a Christian, bro?" I lit into him, "You judge everybody. You walk into church and avoid the people you don't like. You mumble under your breath about 'How irritating' or 'How annoying' people are. Dude, you complain about slow drivers and even slow shopping carts at the store. Everybody is an idiot or a jerk."

He didn't say a word as I continued my full-frontal assault. "You talk a good game but look at your life, man. You counsel guys on how to be God-honoring husbands and you can't make it a week without having a verbal brawl with your wife. I'm surprised she doesn't just pack her bags and leave sometimes. And your own children hardly even talk to you anymore but you think you can school a roomful of men on the finer points of raising kids."

Now I was on a roll, so I kept hammering. "You talk about faith, but every time the money runs low or things don't work out like you want, I half expect you to jettison everything and just walk away from God. You can barely pay the bills half the time and you never even know where the next money is coming from! You're in your fifties and you don't even have a retirement plan, a weekly paycheck or a real job. How can you live like that? You have the audacity to call yourself a man?"

At the end of the character assassination, I decided to move in for the kill. "And look at you, bro. You're overweight, balding, and gray. You were doing great with your gym regimen but you blew it and got out of the habit. And not just working out but your diet and even your Bible disciplines suck." He looked up at me, with his face still half-covered in shaving cream, completely dejected. "But I just got that e-mail from that guy who said he admired how great of a husband and father I am," he objected.

"Really," I retorted, "who do you think you're kidding? That guy just doesn't know you the way I do. If he did, he would probably just stop talking to you altogether. You're nothing more than a wannabe Christian with a cheap plastic cross."

I looked back into the mirror and wiped the excess shaving cream off of my face. Yet another morning facing my own worst enemy—me. Not a day goes by when I wish I hadn't said "that" or done "that." Mornings often consumed by worry and regret detract from the real miracles occurring in my life for many years. My salvation. My rescue from the pit of Hell. The debt was paid in full by Christ on that cross, and now I am free.

Sanctification is a journey. It's a process. And it takes a lifetime and even then, we won't be made perfect until we are in the presence of Jesus Himself, who will be seated on His Throne. I need to stop beating myself every morning and start focusing on how far I've come, not how short I fall.

God is a loving and forgiving Father, not a tyrannical record-keeper. He's altogether good, and altogether Holy, and

He will never beat us up repeatedly about our past. Remember what King David wrote:

He will not always accuse,
nor will he harbor his anger forever;
he does not treat us as our sins deserve
or repay us according to our iniquities.

For as high as the heavens are above the earth,
so great is his love for those who fear him;
as far as the east is from the west,
so far has he removed our transgressions from us.

Psalm 103:9–12

I've heard it said God won't force us to look back and then chastise us with, "Look at what a fool you are. You keep doing the same thing over and over. You're a failure." The only time God makes us look back is to see just how far He's carried us so far. If we are truly in Christ, we have this assurance:

Therefore, there is now no condemnation for those who are in Christ Jesus.

Romans 8:1

So today, I confess I will fail. I will say something stupid or think something even worse. But less for the grace of God go I. It's a new day and His mercies are new again today.

Yesterday has been removed from the record books and God has again pushed the Holy "reset" button.

Maybe this is where you are today. God wants you to know it will all be okay. If you put your foot in your mouth, seek forgiveness. If you feel like you're failing, know this is all part of the process. God didn't lead you into the desert to die. He's got your back and will carry you off the battlefield when life blows your legs off.

So what do we do when everything seems to be collapsing around us? Read these words of Paul:

Do not be anxious about anything, but in every situation, by prayer and petition, with thanksgiving, present your requests to God. And the peace of God, which transcends all understanding, will guard your hearts and your minds in Christ Jesus. Finally, brothers, whatever is true, whatever is noble, whatever is right, whatever is pure, whatever is lovely, whatever is admirable—if anything is excellent or praiseworthy—think about such things.

Philippians 4:4–8

So today, we will:

1. Not be anxious.
2. Pray for God's divine help.
3. Be thankful for what we have.
4. Expect the peace of God, which will transcend our feelings or circumstances, even when we don't see a way out.
5. And finally, if it's not true, right, noble, pure, lovely, admirable, excellent or praiseworthy, we won't waste a moment's time thinking about it.

We won't beat ourselves up this day, because we know Whose we are.

We demolish arguments and every pretension that sets itself up against the knowledge of God, and we take captive every thought to make it obedient to Christ.

2 Corinthians 10:5

Glory to God!

DAY #13

TOUGH DECISIONS AND WISE COUNSEL

"Honey, my car isn't blowing cold anymore," my wife stated as she walked in from the garage, "it's been that way for a while but I didn't want to spend the money to fix it. But it's hot outside now." Hot would be an understatement, considering we live in Southwest Florida and I was amazed she'd lasted as long as she had with her air conditioning blowing hot air on her face whenever she drove. So off I went to the shop to "investigate the problem."

After waiting several hours for "the call," my mechanic said, "Well, it's the evaporator. We will need to access it by removing the entire dashboard. I'm guessing it will cost around $1,800 to fix it." I was speechless. Nearly two thousand dollars to fix a car worth about $2,800 on a good day. "Let me get back to you," I sighed.

Knowing I have some pretty solid business minds on our board of directors, I emailed the three men who had good financial sense and who would likely tell me what I wanted to hear, which was "Buy a new car." I informed them the car was

worth $2,800 and after we put $1,800 into it to fix the air conditioning, it would still be worth exactly $2,800.

The first reply arrived and validated my position. "Your wife
needs to be driving a new car," was the bottom line. Then came
the second reply, which sounded nearly identical to the first.
Finally, after a little delay, the third answer landed in my inbox,
and it started with "You're probably not going to like what I'm
about to say, but . . . ." It was from my battle buddy and accountability partner, David. He recounted no less than ten instances
when God provided for us in the past and finished with, "You
need to fix the car. God will give you a new car when He
is ready."

As much as I didn't want to hear that or spend the money,
I sided with the odd man out and heeded David's counsel.
Why? Because first, he gave it all to God. And just as importantly, I know without a shadow of a doubt he would never steer
me wrong.

King David had a guy like that, named Jonathan. Jonathan
was not only his best friend but also the son of David's predecessor, King Saul, and his brother-in-law. From the beginning,
regardless of Jonathan's family connections, there was a unique
and virtually unbreakable loyalty between Jonathan and his
brother, David.

We first meet Jonathan in 1 Samuel 13, where he attacked
a battalion of Philistines, and by 1 Samuel 14, Jonathan is actually taunting the enemy combatants. After David is anointed as
the king of the future, the young man moves into King Saul's
home and begins serving in the household. Then he meets
Jonathan:

*After David had finished talking with Saul, Jonathan became
one in spirit with David, and he loved him as himself.*

1 Samuel 18:1

The battle-ready brotherhood between David and Jonathan defied even family loyalty, as on more than one instance, Jonathan sided with his friend over his father. And there was never a time when Jonathan steered young David the wrong way.

Saul told his son Jonathan and all the attendants to kill David. But Jonathan had taken a great liking to David and warned him, "My father Saul is looking for a chance to kill you. Be on your guard tomorrow morning; go into hiding and stay there. I will go out and stand with my father in the field where you are. I'll speak to him about you and will tell you what I find out."

1 Samuel 19:1–3

Jonathan was acutely aware David was going to de-throne his father at some point and knew the entire circumstance was ordained and directed by God.

May the Lord be with you as he has been with my father. But show me unfailing kindness like the Lord's kindness as long as I live, so that I may not be killed, and do not ever cut off your kindness from my family—not even when the Lord has cut off every one of David's enemies from the face of the earth."

So Jonathan made a covenant with the house of David, saying, "May the Lord call David's enemies to account." And Jonathan had David reaffirm his oath out of love for him, because he loved him as he loved himself.

1 Samuel 20:13–17

If you're at all familiar with the rest of the story, Jonathan helped David escape his enraged father and later watched as David ascended to the throne of Israel. And when Jonathan falls in battle, King David brings Jonathan's only living son into his house as one of his own family. Even after death, the bond remained.

The Bible mentions just how important it is to seek the counsel of other people:

Where there is no counsel, the people fall; but in the multitude of counselors there is safety.

Proverbs 11:14 NKJV

Without counsel, plans go awry, but in the multitude of counselors they are established.

Proverbs 15:22 NKJV

But here's the catch. It's really easy for us to find people who will agree with our plans. In fact, we can even migrate toward the favorable responses, while disregarding the perspective that contradicts what we want. But often what we want isn't what we need to hear.

Although merely surmised from scriptural timing, it is thought David ran from Saul for around seven years. That's seven years of hiding in caves, living in foreign countries, and running from a man who wanted to kill him. Sure, the warrior named David could have killed Saul any number of times while he served inside his household and even had several opportunities to kill the king during the chase and didn't.

David held to the promise from God, reinforced by his best friend, Jonathan. And David ultimately reigned in Israel for forty years.

Are you facing a major decision you've essentially already made? Did you seek the counsel of others before moving forward? Today, ask God to bring a Jonathan into your life; a man who knows your motives, and seeks the face of the Lord for answers. God often speaks through those He positions around us—men who would never send us down the wrong path. It might be the more difficult option. But it will be worth it.

DAY #14

WAITING FOR A
CLEAR DIRECTION

From the moment young David dropped Goliath the Philistine with a sling and a stone, he was a warrior. At the pinnacle of his career as king and commander, he had a staff of thirty mighty men (2 Samuel 23:8) and over a million soldiers:

And there were in Israel eight hundred thousand valiant men who drew the sword, and the men of Judah were five hundred thousand men.

2 Samuel 24:9 NKJV

In fact, even while running for his life from King Saul, he was a battle-hardened commander to whom soldiers naturally migrated. Even men with nothing else left to live for found themselves drawn to David:

And everyone who was in distress, everyone who was in debt, and everyone who was discontented gathered to him. So he became captain over them. And there were about four hundred men with him.

1 Samuel 22:2 NKJV

David's battle victories are as resounding as they are numerous. As a military commander, he had multiple victories over Israel's arch-enemy, the Philistines, as well as victories over the Geshurites, the Gezrites, the Amalekites (1 Samuel 27:8–9). He crossed swords with the Philistines yet again, who were compelled to team up with the Moabites, Zobah, Syria, and Edom (2 Samuel 8:2), just to have a shot at beating the king of Israel. David led Israel against the Ammonites in 2 Samuel 10 and is again victorious. Believe it or not, King David fights the Philistines another four times in 2 Samuel 21:15–20.

Regardless of his combat acumen, King David was also acutely connected to God. Sure, he messed up just like the rest of us but David was always quick to repent and shift his focus back to the magnitude, grace, mercy, and forgiveness of a Holy God. All you need to do is read David's Psalms to see just how tight he was with the Lord.

Due to the aforementioned connection to God, King David always sought the counsel of the Lord before he made a single military move or entered a conflict.

. . . and David inquired of the LORD, "Shall I pursue this raiding party? Will I overtake them?" "Pursue them," he answered. "You will certainly overtake them and succeed in the rescue."

1 Samuel 30:8

. . . he inquired of the LORD, saying, "Shall I go and attack these Philistines?" The LORD answered him, "Go, attack the Philistines and save Keilah."

1 Samuel 23:2

Although he was likely supremely confident in his own prowess on the battlefield, King David prayed and waited for God's answer. Needless to say, David always seemed to be on the receiving end of the Lord's favor in combat. In fact, he was probably certain enough in his army's penchant for winning he could have easily become over-confident or even presumptuous about his upcoming battles. Well, I've defeated everyone I've asked about, David could have thought, so let's just assume God's with us every time. I don't need to pray any more about this because I always get the same answer. And the victory.

There's one battle in particular where assuming God's favor wouldn't have ended well for King David. It occurred just after his coronation as king of Israel, against his recurring foes from Philistia:

When the Philistines heard that David had been anointed king over Israel, they went up in full force to search for him, but David heard about it and went down to the stronghold. Now the Philistines had come and spread out in the Valley of Rephaim;

2 Samuel 5:17–18

As with previous military engagements, the newly crowned king sought his marching orders from God, and he predictably received the same answer from God

. . . so David inquired of the Lord, "Shall I go and attack the Philistines? Will you deliver them into my hands?" The Lord answered him, "Go, for I will surely deliver the Philistines into your hands."

2 Samuel 5:19

Given the answer he received, David successfully defeated the resilient Philistines in one town but the enemy regrouped a short time later in the Valley of Rephaim. What happens immediately before engaging the enemy a second time is worthy of mention:

. . . so David inquired of the Lord, and he answered, "Do not go straight up, but circle around behind them and attack them in front of the poplar trees. As soon as you hear the sound of marching in the tops of the poplar trees, move quickly, because that will mean the Lord has gone out in front of you to strike the Philistine army."

2 Samuel 5:23–24

Imagine for a moment the potential for defeat had David not sought the plan from God. The king defeated the enemy a few days early, yet David still pressed into the Lord. He never made a move without prayer or obedience:

So David did as the Lord commanded him, and he struck down the Philistines all the way from Gibeon to Gezer.

2 Samuel 5:25

David waited for the God-dictated timing. He broke out his compass and moved in behind the Philistines as he was instructed. Then he waited for the sound of feet in the trees. Had he driven into the enemy head-on, David likely would have suffered defeat.

Because King David sought the counsel of God, his second defeat of the Philistines didn't just clear out the Valley of Rephaim, but drove them out over the roughly eighteen miles between Gibeon and Gezer!

It's amazing how often I get overzealous and make a move with only half of what God is attempting to tell me. Oftentimes, God only gives us the next step. He can see the entire battlefield, while we can only see the tree line.

What is God revealing to you today about the battle in front of you? As I mentioned in chapter 9, battle evolves, and openings appear as God moves the right people or circumstances into the correct positions to assure victory. Are you waiting for His direction? Running out of patience for the battle to finally be won?

God is in the waiting. Listen to His voice. Hold off until you hear His clear and perfect direction. And He will give you a victory that will span from Gibeon to Gezer. In Jesus's Name. Amen.

DAY #15

SUPERFICIAL

A young man walks into the law offices of Joe Miller, a small-time attorney in the big city of Philadelphia. Based upon his cheesy TV commercials, Miller doesn't really appear to be much of a lawyer. The two met only once previously, in a courtroom as "combatants." Now this young man, Andrew Beckett, is in dire need of legal help and Miller is his last option.

It's the mid-1980's and Andrew has just been fired from his long-time career—as an attorney, of all things. Up until a few days before, Beckett was a key player at a large conservative Philadelphia law firm. He was the rising star and a future partner. He was the guy who always got called for the big cases and he had just been summarily fired.

You may recognize this story line as the one from the movie *Philadelphia*, which stars Tom Hanks as Beckett, and Denzel Washington as his not-so-polished attorney. Beckett was indeed fired, and it was cited by his firm that it was largely performance based. But it was, in reality, due to the young man's recent diagnosis with the then-relatively-unknown disease called

AIDS. His firm wanted nothing to do with Andrew's lifestyle or his illness, so they released him as quickly as possible.

As the two attorneys meet and exchange pleasantries, it appears to be the convergence of two legal minds. Beckett gives his prospective attorney the backstory, then discloses the real reason for his sudden termination from the firm. Miller, who seems visibly shaken at the acronym AIDS, states, "Sorry, but I just don't see a case, counselor." Miller is pretty quick to get Beckett out of his office, so he calls an abrupt end to the meeting.

What does the frazzled Miller do the minute Andrew Beckett is gone? He sanitizes his whole office—the stapler, the chair, and anything else the sick man touched. Then he gets on the phone to schedule an immediate doctor's appointment, just to confirm he has not been infected with AIDS. It's really sort of comical, considering we now know HIV can't be transmitted on a Swingline.

Let's take the same scenario and move it into our community of men, both in and out of the church. Not the AIDS part, but Miller's reaction to it. We get together with other men, we sharpen each other, and we pray for each other. At church, we greet men, and we really do want them to be a part of what God is doing. We invite them to small groups, serve with them on the usher team, and go on weekend motorcycle rides.

However, the minute a man in our small group says he is battling pornography, has been swept up in an extramarital affair, lost his job or is in the throes of an unrecoverable marital flatspin, something happens to us. We often involuntarily back away, as if there is some way we are going to catch it. Just like Joe Miller's fear of contracting AIDS from a doorknob, we pull back, sanitize ourselves and often go superficial on the man. At the very moment he needs us most, we freak out and bail out on him.

You know, Jesus made a point of hanging out with the people you and I would be the most likely to run from. Lepers, sick people, losers, rejects—and He simply loved them. He healed blind guys and paralytics, regardless who they were or what their background was. And when confronted about eating with tax collectors and sinners, Jesus quickly set the record straight:

Jesus said to them, "It is not the healthy who need a doctor, but the sick. I have not come to call the righteous, but sinners."

Mark 2:17

Jesus stopped dead in his tracks when a bleeding woman touched the hem of His garment, even though He was actually on His way to heal a man named Jairus's critically ill daughter.

Then a man named Jairus, a synagogue leader, came and fell at Jesus' feet, pleading with him to come to his house because his only daughter, a girl of about twelve, was dying. As Jesus was on his way, the crowds almost crushed him. And a woman was there who had been subject to bleeding for twelve years, but no one could heal her. She came up behind him and touched the edge of his cloak, and immediately her bleeding stopped. "Who touched me?" Jesus asked.

Then the woman, seeing that she could not go unnoticed, came trembling and fell at his feet. In the presence of all the people, she told why she had touched him and how she had been instantly healed. Then he said to her, "Daughter, your faith has healed you. Go in peace."

While Jesus was still speaking, someone came from the house of Jairus, the synagogue leader. "Your daughter is dead," he said. "Don't bother the teacher anymore."

Luke 8:41-45;47–49

Jesus was clearly right in the middle of something very important but He valued that woman enough to take the time to speak with her and to heal her. Public perception of her condition, or His involvement in her problem, was completely irrelevant to Jesus, because He cared enough to backburner everything for one person. And we should be operating the same way.

And, Jairus's daughter died while Jesus was speaking to the woman He just healed.

In John 8, Jesus didn't condemn the adulteress, even though the whole town wanted to stone her to death. It didn't matter if a person was physically ill, the neighborhood reject, or just a societal train wreck, Jesus cared about everybody. And He still does today.

So the next time a close friend tells you his wife is leaving, don't chase the guy out of your office. Divorce isn't contagious, addiction can't be spread by a handshake, and I promise he won't sneeze his cancer all over you.

Get in the game today. Look around at your wife, children, co-workers, and even that random guy at the gas station. Take the time to ask them how they are doing. Listen to their battles. Speak the truth in love. We are never too busy to stop and listen. Or too burdened by the workload of the day to justify walking around a hurting person.

So let's love like Jesus and walk these people through their pain. We may be the only one who stops, asks or appears to care.

Remember: "I tell you the truth, whatever you did for one of the least of these brothers of mine, you did for me."

Matthew 25:40

DAY #16

HOW TO SUCCEED AT CHRISTIANITY WITHOUT REALLY TRYING

Back in the late 1980's, long before I met the Lord, I did a decade-long stint as a landscape guy. I was a lawnmower operator for a large commercial company and I lived my life as most of my colleagues did. My typical day consisted of "Get up at 5 a.m., work until 6 p.m., drink until midnight, pass out, repeat." Other than the occasional night that carried into the morning, where I often went straight from drinking to working, that was my life.

And like every guy, I think I got to a point where I thought "There has GOT to be more to life than this." After all, I was in my twenties, I had a girlfriend of sorts, and an apartment. According to the world, I was a man, I suppose. During the early part of my landscape career, I worked side-by-side with a man named Bruce, who was an overtly born-again believer. At some point every single day, he would tell me I needed Jesus. Of course, back then, my immediate thought was "Jesus who"? Given my non-faith upbringing, I had virtually no idea who Jesus was. But day after day, Bruce kept on me.

Since he was stuck in the truck next to me day in and day out, I finally began questioning Bruce about life, space, Noah's ark, creation—anything that popped into my head. He did a great job of answering all my questions, so finally, during one of our typical lunch-in-the-truck moments, I decided to ask him about marriage. After a little pause, Bruce flatly told me, as part of following Jesus, he and his wife felt sex was strictly for procreation. He concluded his ten-minute answer by stating, since they were done having kids, he hadn't touched his wife in over twelve years.

And thus marks the abrupt end to what we'll call: "Exploring Christianity with Bruce."

Fast forward to 2007. Now saved and serving the Lord in ministry, I was tasked as the master of ceremonies at Christian men's events all over Florida. As one particular event was about to commence, I was preparing to take the stage and launch into eight hours of sheer, unabashed manliness.

At zero hour, two older (much older) men approached me, wagging their fingers angrily at the stage and shouting, "You can't have drums on the platform! It's not Christian!" After digging deep into the dark recesses of my somewhat new Old Testament knowledge, I informed them King David danced naked, and we would be doing the same thing during the afternoon session. And thus marks the abrupt end to "My conversation with two old dudes about drums."

As I look back at my well-over-thirty years of living my life without Jesus and why I justified living in the world was better than the Christian alternative, I can narrow the main reasons down to just a few simple points.

First, Christianity was all sacrifice and everyone who went to church was beyond dull. I felt, at this time in my life, a man had to jettison anything fun in order to be Christian. Second, and perhaps even more importantly, was every Christian man I encountered was "man repellent." And utterly hypocritical. I didn't see anything in them I wanted, so I avoided them all. Ultimately, as many non-believers do, I came to the conclusion I didn't need coats and ties, pipe organs or pews to live a fulfilling life.

Notice, God isn't anywhere in that conclusion above, nor is Jesus Christ. But that was my reality. And it honestly still is for a lot of guys we meet, work with or workout with, every day of the week.

So how does a man succeed at Christianity without repelling everyone we meet along the way? Although we've complicated much of it with "in-house" arguments about worship music styles, pews versus chairs, pre versus post-millennial rapture, and using the King James or the NIV, it really is quite simple.

Back it up two thousand years and let's take it from Jesus and the Apostle Paul. Here are three simple guidelines that will make life as a believer easier and maybe even lead a man who isn't saved right to the foot of the cross.

1. It's all about love. Jesus gave us the "two greatest Commandments," right?

   "Love the Lord your God with all your heart and with all your soul and with all your mind." This is the first and greatest commandment. And the second is like it: "Love your neighbor as yourself." All the Law and the Prophets hang on these two commandments."

   Matthew 22:37-40

   When in doubt, love. When the guy in the car next to you cuts you off, love him. It isn't about wardrobe, doctrine, music, Bible translations or pews. Jesus narrowed all the rules into one word: Love!

2. Live life as a paradox. Think backward to live forward. If the world tells you it's right, it's probably wrong.

Love your enemies:

But I tell you, love your enemies and pray for those who persecute you.

Matthew 5:44

When we are weak, He is strong:

That is why, for Christ's sake, I delight in weaknesses, in insults, in hardships, in persecutions, in difficulties. For when I am weak, then I am strong.

2 Corinthians 12:10

We must die to live:

For if you live according to the flesh, you will die; but if by the Spirit you put to death the misdeeds of the body, you will live.

Romans 8:13

For to me, to live is Christ and to die is gain.—Philippians 1:21

3. Edify, don't destroy. Speak life into everyone you meet today.

Do not let any unwholesome talk come out of your mouths, but only what is helpful for building others up according to their needs, that it may benefit those who listen.

Ephesians 4:29

When you want to level someone with your tongue, just don't.

If anyone considers himself religious and yet does not keep a tight rein on his tongue, he deceives himself and his religion is worthless.

James 1:26

I don't know about you, but my mouth gets me in a lot of trouble.

The tongue has the power of life and death, and those who love it will eat its fruit.

Proverbs 18:21

With the tongue we praise our Lord and Father, and with it we curse human beings, who have been made in God's likeness. Out of the same mouth come praise and cursing. My brothers and sisters, this should not be. Can both fresh water and salt water flow from the same spring? My brothers, can a fig tree bear olives, or a grapevine bear figs? Neither can a salt spring produce fresh water.

James 3:9–12

The three principles can be used anywhere, any time. Apply them to any situation.

Has there been a communication breakdown with your wife? Love her, serve her, love God with everything you have, and speak kindly to her regardless what she said.

Does your boss at work make you feel like quitting? Love him, work hard, love God with everything you have, and watch what you say.

Are the kids out of control? Love them, love God with everything you have, and don't exasperate them with your words.

It's really as simple as 1, 2, 3. Love, serve, and edify. And guys, living their lives like I used to live, will see something in you they desperately want. They will see Jesus in you.

Now, if you're anything like I am right about now, God has already placed someone on your heart. Perhaps it's a co-worker, or maybe it's someone a little closer to home. Set down offense, seek forgiveness or extend it, then love them, die to self and build them up. You will be surprised just how powerful loving like Jesus can be in the lives of those around us.

Most important of all, continue to show deep love for each other, for love covers a multitude of sins.

1 Peter 4:8

DAY #17

STRIVING IS
OVERRATED

For most of my time as a believer, I've had another Christian man in my life to support me, encourage me, and hold me accountable. In a practical sense, this is what you'd call "peer-to-peer accountability." We are at the same stage in life, with adult children, careers, marriages, and consequently, we get to walk each other through the battlefield of life. I also spend quite a bit of time interacting with younger men, as they drive headlong into college choices, careers, weddings, and babies. As you'd expect, God uses my successes and failures as a father, husband, and man of God to help guide these young men through life. Practically, this would be something akin to a "superior/subordinate accountability." In a Biblical model, the first man mentioned above would be similar to a "Paul and Silas" relationship, while the second man would definitely be a "Paul and Timothy" guy. Someone I'm actively mentoring.

Unfortunately, I've had a glaringly obvious hole in my walk with Christ. The gap has gone largely unchecked for over fifteen years. In point of fact, I've been missing an older man pouring into me. A mentor. Someone who's already walked through seasons of life as a grandfather, empty nester, and seasoned husband with decades more experience than I have. In the Bible, this man would be "Barnabas." And it wasn't until just recently, upon the urging of my wife and the counsel of an Air Force chaplain friend, God put my Barnabas in my life.

One thing about mentors is they ask hard questions. The kind of difficult questions, quite frankly, even more difficult to answer. You see, I've been struggling with the work of ministry. I guess you could even say there are times when I spend time more time working "on" the ministry than actively "in" the ministry. Maybe you've been there in your walk with Jesus. Suddenly it's less like climbing Mt. Everest and more like driving through Kansas—miles of flat ground. The fire has slowly dimmed from where it once was. But truthfully, that is not where Jesus wants us. Sure, I know what I'd tell my "Timothy," but I was stuck with the inability to fix myself. Because of this, the first discussion I had with my "Barnabas" revolved around a kind of Christian burnout. He is a fifty-year ministry veteran and I just knew he could shed some light on why I was so tired and "dry."

Instead of giving me a mini-sermon, he instead gave me homework. The objective before our next meeting was to read the first fifteen chapters of the Gospel of John, noting what does or does not make a disciple. Within those chapters, I certainly found what Jesus says about what it takes to be a disciple; but I found something else. I discovered, in large part, why I felt spiritually "off the rails," so to speak. There's a great overview of "spiritual disconnect" in the Gospel of Luke:

As Jesus and his disciples were on their way, he came to a village where a woman named Martha opened her home to him. She had a sister called Mary, who sat at the Lord's feet listening to what he said. But Martha was distracted by all the preparations that had to be made. She came to him and asked, "Lord, don't you care that my sister has left me to do the work by myself? Tell her to help me!"

"Martha, Martha," the Lord answered, "you are worried and upset about many things, but few things are needed—or indeed only one. Mary has chosen what is better, and it will not be taken away from her."

Luke 10:38–42

While Martha was frantically running around, Mary just sat there at the feet of Jesus, listening. And as I read through my "homework," God revealed my entire problem within the first sixteen verses of John 15:

I am the true vine, and My Father is the vinedresser. Every branch in Me that does not bear fruit He takes away; and every branch that bears fruit He prunes, that it may bear more fruit. You are already clean because of the word which I have spoken to you. Abide in Me, and I in you. As the branch cannot bear fruit of itself, unless it abides in the vine, neither can you, unless you abide in Me.

I am the vine, you are the branches. He who abides in Me, and I in him, bears much fruit; for without Me you can do nothing. If anyone does not abide in Me, he is cast out as a branch and is withered; and they gather them and throw them into the fire, and they are burned. If you abide in Me, and My words abide in you, you will ask what you desire, and it shall be done for you. By this My Father is glorified, that you bear much fruit; so you will be My disciples.

John 15:1–8 NKJV

Simply put, God is the gardener and Jesus is the vine. God prunes off any part of the vine that doesn't bear fruit and prunes the fruitful parts of the vine to produce even more fruit (notice Jesus says "*Every branch in me*"). So the bad news is, if we aren't bearing fruit, God might just prune us out of the picture. But there's more to the story, and our mission.

Jesus goes on to give us the solution to our Spiritual dry spells. He simply says "Abide in me." The archaic definition of the word "Abide" reads "continue without fading or being lost" and "live or dwell." We must live within the Vine to continue to bear fruit, because "a branch cannot bear fruit by itself" and we, as believers, cannot bear fruit unless we abide in Him.

The verses above close with an encouragement for those of us who've grown weary. If we live attached to Jesus and we fill ourselves with His Word, we will pray and God will answer. The end result? God is glorified when we bear fruit (grow His Kingdom) and we are unquestionably His disciples.

But there's more . . .

As the Father loved Me, I also have loved you; abide in My love. If you keep My commandments, you will abide in My love, just as I have kept My Father's commandments and abide in His love.

John 15:9 NKJV

You are My friends if you do whatever I command you.

John 15:14 NKJV

You did not choose Me, but I chose you and appointed you that you should go and bear fruit, and that your fruit should remain, that whatever you ask the Father in My name He may give you.

John 15:16 NKJV

Verse 9 is, first, a reminder we are loved and we absolutely need to stay connected to Jesus to accomplish anything. It's a not-so-subtle reminder to obey God's commandments as an integral part of the process of "abiding." The result is the Master calls us a "friend."

God's entire purpose for us is to bear fruit—to see a commensurate return both in us and for the kingdom. We didn't choose Him. He chose us. That, my brothers is the highest calling anyone can have. The Creator of the universe, the Author and Perfecter of our faith, has called us to be His disciples.

Are you in a spiritual desert right now? Maybe we've mastered all of the disciplines of a disciple, but we are running around like Martha?

Today, get re-attached to the Vine. Take time over the next day or two to read through the first fifteen chapters of John for yourself. Look for the words within the Word that spell out what we must do as men to be His disciples.

Spoiler alert: It starts with setting aside the striving and instead simply abiding.

No amount of striving can ever replace the simple joys of spending time in the Word with our Savior, Jesus. Abiding always comes before the fruit. So take a seat at His feet.

DAY #18

ABOUT THE FATHER'S BUSINESS

Having spent the past fifteen years in vocational ministry with no other source of income, I've learned the value other people. I've also learned to shelve my pride, which is typically the first thing to get attacked when part of your very survival is reliant upon the generosity of other people. Sure, we have income from speaking engagements and book sales, but over a third of our annual ministry income comes from men who've committed to standing behind the value of men in the family. Frankly, I wouldn't be able to do what I do without guys like them. I even had one man tell me, "Don't ever remind me and don't ever thank me. God didn't give me the ability to speak or write but He did give me the ability to make a lot of money. My role in the kingdom is to support men like you." The amazing part of our life in ministry is I haven't missed a meal yet!

When Paul began his mission trips with Barnabas and then Silas, he had no real source of income. He was a tentmaker (and professional Pharisee) by trade, but he did have a team of people funding the majority of his work. While he rarely accepted money from those he was ministering to, the church in Antioch played a vital role in "sending" Paul and his compatriots. Paul spoke of ministry in his first letter to Timothy as well:

The elders who direct the affairs of the church well are worthy of double honor, especially those whose work is preaching and teaching. For Scripture says, "Do not muzzle an ox while it is treading out the grain," and "The worker deserves his wages."

1 Timothy 5:17–18

If you've been in church more than one time, there's a strong probability you've heard the tithing message. It's usually anchored with Scripture designed to convict instead of inspire:

Will a man rob God?
Yet you have robbed Me!
But you say,
'In what way have we robbed You?'
In tithes and offerings.

Malachi 3:8 NKJV

It doesn't inspire one to be a cheerful giver, does it? As a professional in ministry, I have to dedicate at least one devotion to the often-maligned topic of tithing. Don't shut the book yet, because this will change the way you view investing in ministry.

Let's set the stage. Even when I wasn't saved, I was pretty familiar with the Nativity story, through movies like *A Charlie Brown Christmas*. Bethlehem, mangers, and three wise men were a Christmas staple in my house, even though we didn't attend church.

In Luke 2, we read about a call for a census, issued by Caesar Augustus where everyone had to return to the city of their birth for a headcount. The purpose of the census was to make certain everyone living within the Roman Empire was paying their appropriate taxes. Since Mary, the soon-to-be mother of Jesus, was marred to Joseph from Bethlehem, they packed up their belongings and headed to the husband's hometown.

The only accommodations they could find for the census was a barn, where Mary gave birth to the Savior. We all know the story, more than likely.

A week after Jesus's birth, Mary and Joseph took their baby to the Temple in Jerusalem for the dedication of the firstborn, and for Mary's purification rites (which was to occur seven days after birth).

When the time came for the purification rites required by the Law of Moses, Joseph and Mary took him to Jerusalem to present him to the Lord (as it is written in the Law of the Lord, "Every first-born male is to be consecrated to the Lord"), and to offer a sacrifice in keeping with what is said in the Law of the Lord: "a pair of doves or two young pigeons."

Luke 2:22–24

Joseph and Mary were considered to be some of the poorest in the area and it's confirmed by their offering. A typical purification offering, set forth in Levitical law, was a lamb. But in cases of extreme financial hardship, God allowed amendments to the required offerings:

But if she cannot afford a lamb, she is to bring two doves or two young pigeons, one for a burnt offering and the other for a sin offering. In this way the priest will make atonement for her, and she will be clean.

Leviticus 12:8

Sometime after Jesus's birth and dedication, Mary and Joseph are visited by the Magi. Remember, the Magi came with camels loaded with gold and rare spices for the Savior of the world. They were also given secret orders by Herod to give up the location of Jesus, because the king planned to kill all of the male children born on the night the Magi first noted the star over Jesus. The Magi knew who Jesus was, and opted to ignore the king's order.

When [the Magi] saw the star, they were overjoyed. On coming to the house, they saw the child with his mother Mary, and they bowed down and worshiped him. Then they opened their treasures and presented him with gifts of gold, frankincense, and myrrh. And having been warned in a dream not to go back to Herod, they returned to their country by another route.

When they had gone, an angel of the Lord appeared to Joseph in a dream. "Get up," he said, "take the child and his mother and escape to Egypt. Stay there until I tell you, for Herod is going to search for the child to kill him."

So he got up, took the child and his mother during the night and left for Egypt, where he stayed until the death of Herod.

Matthew 2:10–14

How does a couple who couldn't even afford an offering sheep live in Egypt for an extended period of time?

As soon as the Magi presented all their gifts to Jesus and left town, the angel told Joseph to flee with the baby. And the young couple, who two weeks before had nothing, now had the means to leave the country.

The Magi likely had no idea their gifts would fund Joseph and Mary's flight from Israel, potentially saving the life of the Savior Jesus.

We never know whose life will change by our obedience to get involved in the Father's business. Our job is to just be obedient in our giving and leave the results to God.

How have you viewed tithing in the past? Do you tithe to your church with the same discipline as other Spiritual disciplines? Today, ask God to show you just how to be a truly joyful giver and maybe even bless you with an opportunity to see how your obedience has affected so many for the kingdom.

Your tithes and offerings can change the world.

DAY #19

COMMUNICATION BREAKDOWN

As you may recall from earlier, there was a painfully long season where I didn't hear from my son, Jordan, very much. In fact, during much of this period of our lives, we neither heard from him nor did we even know where he was living. Other than an occasional awkward and somewhat strained phone call, I didn't see him. The lack of interaction affected everything in our house, including my normally-gracious wife, Joni. Even the mention of his name would cause the heartache to gradually morph into anger in Joni and me. And with Joni's protective streak, when I hurt, she tends to jump to my defense pretty quickly.

So when the phone rang and the caller ID showed his name, I instinctively tensed up. "I wonder what he wants," was typically my first thought, because there was often an ulterior motive masked within the random phone call. This time, it was no different.

"Hey Dad," my son greeted me. "How's it going, son?" was my typical reply. As was our normal back then, there was no dancing around or casual talking, and Jordan went directly to the ask. "I found a car I'd like to buy with the money Mom left me when she passed away and I don't know anything about cars. Would you be able to meet me at the car lot to take a look and let me know if it's a good deal?"

"Sure, son," I replied, "where is it?" As it turned out, it was a solid hour from my house to the car lot. I honestly don't recall where he was living at the time, but apparently it was halfway. So I stopped what I was doing, grabbed my keys and headed to the garage.

"Where are you going? Was that Jordan?" Joni inquired, already knowing the answer. "Yeah," I responded, giving her the condensed version of his request for help looking at the car. My wife, a bit taken aback, and a little protective stated the obvious: "He always asks you to do stuff and you just drop everything and respond. We can't even get him to come over on holidays and you just run off when he calls."

You know what? She was right. As I began driving to the car lot, resentment built deep within my heart. I spent nearly thirty minutes talking to myself, "Yeah! She's right! Why do I always do this?!," followed by a long list of "When he asked, I should have said . . . " responses. Then I started to pray out loud, over the loud music in my car. "God," I prayed, "Bring my son back! Why does he only care about me when he needs a favor?" Then I punctuated the prayer with the statement, "He only calls me when he needs something!"

I abruptly stopped praying, and over the noise of my car and the radio, I clearly heard God whisper, "David. You do the same thing to me."

The very thing that drove me absolutely nuts about my son; I was doing to God. Suddenly humbled, I thought of my prayer life. I pondered the number of 9-1-1 prayers I fired to the throne room, never once saying "Thank you" and rarely, if ever, just sitting down to catch up with God. Always a motive or need; never a relationship.

That moment changed my prayer life and my awareness of God's need to hear from me. We are His creation, and He really and truly desires to commune with us. Sure, God wants to hear our petitions, but He also wants ALL of us. Think about how many times we read in His Word of times when God just wanted to spend time with people. Adam and Eve walked with God in the Garden of Eden (Genesis 3:8), Noah *walked faithfully with God*" Genesis 6:9, Abram walked with God, *Enoch walked with God* Genesis 5:22 and Moses routinely met God face to face: *The LORD would speak to Moses face to face, as one speaks to a friend,* Exodus 33:11.

It's clearly important to God that we simply walk with Him, even if we don't have the chance to do it in person as the patriarchs in the Old Testament did. In fact, we have something the founders of the faith didn't. We have direct access to the kingdom through Jesus Christ:

My dear children, I am writing this to you so that you will not sin. But if anyone does sin, we have an advocate who pleads our case before the Father. He is Jesus Christ, the one who is truly righteous.

1 John 2:1 NLT

How many friends do you have who would be willing to sacrifice their own child just to secure a relationship with you? God did precisely that:

For God so loved the world that he gave his one and only Son, that whoever believes in him shall not perish but have eternal life.

John 3:16

While He walked the earth for those thirty-three years, Jesus made it abundantly clear the type of relationship we have available with our Savior:

No longer do I call you servants, for the servant does not know what his master is doing; but I have called you friends, for all that I have heard from my Father I have made known to you.

John 15:15

I really hope I'm not the only guy out there who goes through long periods of prayer drought. Maybe you've gotten in the "emergency prayer" mode or the "little kid's Christmas list prayer" mode? Or maybe prayer can just be awkward or difficult because you just have no idea what to say.

Remember this: He's the Creator of the universe but He is also our Daddy:

The Spirit you received does not make you slaves, so that you live in fear again; rather, the Spirit you received brought about your adoption to sonship. And by him we cry, "Abba, Father."

Romans 8:15

Today, I'm going to encourage you to use a prayer model that always re-centers my efforts to connect with a God whose heart is to connect with us. It's called the **ACTS** model of prayer and it will change how you pray:

A—Adoration (You are great and mighty, our Shield, our Rock . . .)

C—Confession (Fill in the blank with everything the Holy Spirit points out)

T—Thanksgiving (All the things He has done for you and given you)

S—Supplication (This is finally where we bring our petitions before Him—the asking)

Notice, it takes a while to get to the list of needs? When we focus our attention on the magnitude of our great God and His Son, Jesus Christ, at the beginning, our prayer needs become secondary to His forgiveness and His blessings on our lives.

Try it this morning. Then set aside a little time first thing every morning to meet with God, just as Moses and Abraham did. Catch Him up on what's going on. He misses you. So make that call today and never hang up on the Father.

Pray without ceasing.   1 Thessalonians 5:17 KJV

DAY #20

NO JOY: WHY MARRIAGE COMMUNICATIONS FALL APART

"No Joy": From military aviation. A pilot reports "no joy" when an attempt to establish visual or radio contact with another aircraft is unsuccessful.

In my first book, *Rough Cut Men*, I spend time introducing something I called your "story." Not to be confused with your testimony, our story is a distorted view of how we see ourselves, based upon the interactions we've had with other people our entire lives.

The first chapter in our story is traditionally penned by our parents, since they are the first people we truly engage with. Believe it not, as we move through life, we continually seek out ways to validate our story, even though the story itself is usually an abject lie of the enemy. I've discovered that even the most seasoned believers often carry the burden of a bad story and it impacts everything from work to parenting. And more importantly, our story can utterly ruin healthy communication between a husband and a wife. In my own life, I've discovered many of my responses to my wife are fueled by dysfunction in my heart and mind because of my stories.

One pervasive story that often rematerializes is "I'm not good enough." That story began when I was seven and I failed to do something correctly my father asked me to do. As a teenager, my grades were never quite good enough. And, as with many people, one bad work e-mail or phone call would again solidify my story of constantly letting people down. No matter how hard I tried to be a good student or a good employee, I fell flat. My "truth" was, I am never good enough, and it all started with my dad. And I could always find ways to reassure myself that my story was indeed true. Ultimately, that "truth" invaded my marriage in a covert, but powerful way.

There have been countless opportunities to distort my marriage with my story of "I'm not good enough." One instance I remember specifically centered around some Ikea furniture. Our son literally outgrew his bedroom in the span of a summer and we opted to buy new furniture. If you know anything about Ikea, most of their furniture comes in little boxes and they give "some assembly required" a whole new meaning.

Upon bringing the new dressers, bed, and desk boxes home, they made it as far as the garage, where they remained for several months. On the day in question, I'd just returned from Los Angeles on a redeye flight, so needless to say I was already sleep deprived and a little compromised. I was sitting at the dining room table, sorting through a week's worth of receipts and mail, when, from the kitchen behind me, I heard my wife ask, "I don't suppose you feel like putting together any furniture today, do you?" After a few moments of searching for the appropriate reply, I instead blew up all over my wife.

Now, I don't know if you've ever been in a position like that, but my response to a relatively simple request was wildly inappropriate. And here's why: I wasn't responding to my wife. I was responding to my story. What she asked was, "Can you put that bedroom furniture together?" What I heard was, "Honey, no matter how well you provide and solid you are as a husband, you still haven't done that furniture. You're never good enough."

Maybe you heard "Why can't you be more like your sister?" or "I wish I'd never had you" from a parent. Perhaps you never heard "I love you" from a mom or dad. Or like me, you are your own worst critic, thinking *I'll never be good enough or smart enough or as good as that other family at church.*

These lies come directly from our story. And straight from the enemy of our souls. And the result is we often do the most damage to the ones closest to us, especially our wives. Sometimes, our filter through which we hear our wives is based upon a story we carry around about who we think we are, not who God says we are. So first, here are a couple of reminders about how God asks us to respond to our helpmate.

May your fountain be blessed, and may you rejoice in the wife of your youth.

Proverbs 5:18

Enjoy life with your wife, whom you love.

Ecclesiastes 9:9a

Submit to one another out of reverence for Christ.

Ephesians 5:21

Husbands, love your wives, just as Christ loved the church and gave himself up for her.

Ephesians 5:25

Husbands, in the same way be considerate as you live with your wives, and treat them with respect as the weaker partner and as heirs with you of the gracious gift of life, so that nothing will hinder your prayers.

1 Peter 3:7

When we read these Scriptures, it can seem like a daunting task if we've got bad communication channels open with our bride. Maybe years of broadcasting in the wrong frequency, simply because we hear her through our story has resulted in a slow erosion to the marriage. Abrupt responses, short answers and replying based on a lie have all made the daily communication challenging. And it's all centered around a lie.

The only way to defeat a lie, is with the truth. You can't have two opposing truths about the same thing and God's Truth found in His Word is our only truth source. So today, I want to remind you instead of the truth of who God says we are. If you allow God's Word to replace the lie, He can also heal damaged hearts, restore broken marriages, and adjust the way we communicate with our wives. And it starts with destroying a bad story.

No matter what anyone has ever said to you, whether it be a parent, a former girlfriend or even your wife, remember:

You can't be worthless and be the price of one Son of God. You can't *"do everything wrong," and be fearfully and wonderfully made.*

Psalm 139:14

You can't believe the lie that you're unlovable when God says, *I have loved you with an everlasting love; I have drawn you with unfailing kindness.*

Jeremiah 31:3

You can't believe everyone leaves you when God says, *Never will I leave you; never will I forsake you.*

Hebrews 13:5

Perhaps you had a parent leave when you were younger and you've been blaming yourself for so long that it's become your truth, when God's truth says *Even if my father and mother abandon me, the LORD cares for me.*

Psalm 27:10 CSB

To rewire communication with our wives, we have to defeat the lie we believe. We will only accomplish that by replacing lies with the truth of God's Word. Take a half an hour this week and write down three or four memories that continually come back to you. It doesn't matter if it's a happy memory or a not-so-good moment. You will likely find these anchor memories point to a lie you believe about yourself. Share it with your battle buddies. Pray God shows you where you may be seeing yourself in a way that doesn't align with how He sees you. Speak the truth over yourself every morning. Replace "I screwed up again" with "I'm a son of the Most High God."

As God reveals our true identity in Christ, free from the clutter of what others have said about us our entire life, it liberates us to hear our wives clearly. If the Holy Spirit has convicted you about something you've said to your wife this week, make it right. And remember . . .

Know this, my beloved brothers: let every person be quick to hear, slow to speak, slow to anger;

James 1:19 ESV

You are fearfully and wonderfully made, the apple of God's eye, and His warrior. You are heirs with Christ. You are a mighty man of God, and you are loved with an everlasting love. God loves you. Walk in His power and love your wife like there's no tomorrow. Then, if tomorrow comes, love her more.

DAY #21

WHO'S MY NEIGHBOR?

O ne of my personal struggles, that comes along with a speaking ministry, is what I call the "after event." The after event is the period of time after I step down from speaking and move to a book table. Due to my transparency about my own failures and struggles, many of the men migrate toward my table to flip through the pages of the book and engage me in conversation.

What begins as nothing more than casual conversation often moves to more pressing issues of each guy who walks up. The struggle part for me is I'm exhausted after, in some cases, eight straight hours of speaking, coupled with a very fast-paced travel schedule involving airports, planes, and rental cars.

To be brutally honest, it gets challenging to keep my attention on the person speaking to me while thinking about crashing face down into a hotel room pillow. And ironically, given the primary objective of the *Rough Cut Men* "Movie Experience" is to get men to talk about what's really going on in their lives, the flesh in me just wants to shut my brain down at a moment when a man is the most vulnerable. I can't be the only guy who feels like this sometimes.

In Luke 10: 25–37, we encounter a conversation between Jesus and an "expert in the law" (likely meaning he has memorized every part of the Old Testament and keeps every single mandate set down in it). You may recognize this as "The Parable of the Good Samaritan":

On one occasion an expert in the law stood up to test Jesus. "Teacher," he asked, "what must I do to inherit eternal life?"

"What is written in the Law?" he replied. "How do you read it?"

He answered, "Love the Lord your God with all your heart and with all your soul and with all your strength and with all your mind; and, Love your neighbor as yourself."

"You have answered correctly," Jesus replied. "Do this and you will live."

But he wanted to justify himself, so he asked Jesus, "And who is my neighbor?"

In reply Jesus said: "A man was going down from Jerusalem to Jericho, when he was attacked by robbers. They stripped him of his clothes, beat him and went away, leaving him half dead. A priest happened to be going down the same road, and when he saw the man, he passed by on the other side. So too, a Levite, when he came to the place and saw him, passed by on the other side. But a Samaritan, as he traveled, came where the man was; and when he saw him, he took pity on him. He went to him and bandaged his wounds, pouring on oil and wine. Then he put the man on his own donkey, brought him to an inn and took care of him. The next day he took out two denarii and gave them to the innkeeper. 'Look after him,' he said, 'and when I return, I will reimburse you for any extra expense you may have.'

"Which of these three do you think was a neighbor to the man who fell into the hands of robbers?"

The expert in the law replied, "The one who had mercy on him."

Jesus told him, "Go and do likewise."

Luke 10:25–37

Here are a couple things to set the stage for today's devotional. Interestingly Jesus never really clearly states why the priest and the Levite avoided the half dead victim by walking on the other side of the road. Back in the time when this occurred, the road between Jerusalem and Jericho was heavily traveled, because Jerusalem was a city of frequent worship and celebration. It was actually more like a mountain path, peppered with caves, with an elevation drop between the two cities of around 3,000 vertical feet.

There's a good chance robbers often hid in those caves, attacking innocent people traveling into the "big city." Maybe the priest and the Levite didn't want to fall victim to a gang of marauders while helping someone else? Or maybe, given that one is the pastor and the other an elder, they were in a hurry to get somewhere. For whatever reason, neither stopped to help.

Then along comes the Samaritan man who not only takes pity on him but bandages his wounds, puts him in a hotel room, and even tells the innkeeper to "run a tab" and the Samaritan would pay upon his return to town.

After telling the parable, Jesus asks a single question to the expert of the law, *Which of these three do you think was a neighbor to the man who fell into the hands of robbers? v 36*

This was probably a very painful moment for the expert because he was a Jew and the Jewish people didn't even acknowledge Samaritans existed. In the eyes of the expert, the Samaritan was no better than a junkyard dog. Today, the term "good Samaritan" is cultural phrase, like "The Golden Rule." You read in the newspaper of a good Samaritan helping his neighbor. But a Jew would never speak of a Samaritan. In fact, when walking through Israel, Jews would actually walk around the entire region of Samaria just so their feet wouldn't touch Samaritan dirt.

Consequently, when Jesus asked the expert who the neighbor was, the Jew answered by saying, *The one who had mercy on him. v 37.* The expert in the law even refuses to say "the Samaritan," opting instead for "the one."

If we are truly honest with ourselves, we have moments like this. Whether a homeless guy at that same traffic light every morning or that person who blows up our phone with drama-filled text messages all the time. Every day, God places opportunities in front of us to love our neighbor, whether they're "our kind" or not. Because of this fact, I want to leave you with Jesus's strategy for loving our neighbor, straight from the playbook of the good Samaritan. Remember, our neighbor, as clearly defined by Jesus in His parable, now officially means everybody.

Five Steps to Loving Your Neighbor

1. Open Your Eyes: The Samaritan saw the wounded man. He saw the need right in front of him. (v 33)
2. Open Your Heart: The Samaritan man took pity on the wounded man. (v 33)
3. Open Your Hands: The Samaritan gave the wounded man aid right there. (v 34)
4. Open Your Schedule: Neither the priest nor the Levite stopped. Regardless the urgency of his calendar, the Samaritan stopped and cared for the wounded man. He was

traveling somewhere, but the Samaritan's destination became second to helping the victim. Not only that, the Samaritan loaded the wounded man onto his donkey and took him to a place to recover.

5. Open Your Wallet: The Samaritan paid for the wounded man's accommodations and promised to cover any subsequent charges during his recovery.

Unbelievably, we are still talking about the Samaritan man 2,000 plus years later. His one selfless act is our benchmark when we see others in need.

Today, open your eyes a little wider. See the need. Help the helpless. Love them by investing your time and your money. We may be the only Jesus they see today.